Joseph Barber Lightfoot, Joseph Barber Lightfoot

Sermons

Joseph Barber Lightfoot, Joseph Barber Lightfoot
Sermons
ISBN/EAN: 9783743451605
Manufactured in Europe, USA, Canada, Australia, Japa
Cover: Foto ©Thomas Meinert / pixelio.de

Manufactured and distributed by brebook publishing software (www.brebook.com)

Joseph Barber Lightfoot, Joseph Barber Lightfoot

Sermons

THE CONTEMPORARY PULPIT LIBRARY.

SERMONS

BY THE LATE RIGHT REV.

J. B. LIGHTFOOT, D.D., D.C.L.,

LORD BISHOP OF DURHAM.

NEW YORK:
THOMAS WHITTAKER,
2 AND 3, BIBLE HOUSE.
1890.

CONTENTS.*

	PAGE
BETHEL	1
THE CONSCIOUSNESS OF SIN HEAVEN'S PATHWAY	17
THE HISTORY OF ISRAEL AN ARGUMENT IN FAVOUR OF CHRISTIANITY	29
THE VISION OF GOD	43
THE HEAVENLY TEACHER	55
CHRISTIANITY AND PAGANISM. I.	65
,, ,, ,, II.	83
,, ,, ,, III.	100
WOMAN AND THE GOSPEL	116
PILATE	129
THE PHARISEE AND THE PUBLICAN	145
OUR CITIZENSHIP	157
AMBITION	170

* *These sermons are printed from reporter's notes.*

Sermons

BY THE LATE

RIGHT REV. J. B. LIGHTFOOT, D.D., D.C.L.,
Lord Bishop of Durham.

BETHEL.*

"Surely the Lord is in this place, and I knew it not."—GEN. xxviii. 16.

An unobtrusive, unimpressive scene, almost indistinguishable, even to the curious eye of the archæologist, "in the maze of undistinguished hills which encompass it"—with nothing to attract the eye, and nothing to fire the imagination; large slabs of bare rock traversed by a well-worn thoroughfare; "no religio loci, no awful shades, no lofty hills." So is the site of Bethel described by the modern traveller. Yet this was none other than the House of God; this was the very gate of heaven.

An unimpressive scene in itself, but appearing still more commonplace, when contrasted with the famous shrines of heathendom—the rock fortress of the Athene, or the pleasant groves of Daphne, or the cloven peak of Parnassus, or the sea-girt

* Preached at Cambridge, Oct. 23rd, 1881.

sanctuary of Delos. No beauty, no grandeur, nothing of loveliness and nothing of awe, nothing exceptional of any kind which can explain or justify its selection. Was there not ground for the wanderer's surprise on that memorable night? Why should this one spot be chosen to plant the foot of the ladder which connected heaven and earth? Why in this bleak wilderness? Why amidst these bare rocks? Why here of all places in the world? Yes, why here?

The paradox of Bethel is the paradox of the Gospel—is the paradox of God's spiritual dispensations at all times. The Incarnation itself was the supreme manifestation of this paradox. The building up of the Church was the proper sequel to the Incarnation.

Look at the accompaniments of the Incarnation. Could any environment of circumstances well have been imagined more incongruous, more alien to this unique event in human history, this supreme revelation of God's wisdom, and power, and beneficence? An obscure corner of the Roman world—an insignificant and down-trodden race, scorned and hated by the rest of mankind—an ox-stall for a nursery, and a carpenter's shop for a school—what is wanting to complete the paradox? Yes, there is still one feature to be added to the picture—the crowning incongruity of all—the felon's death on the cross. Said not the prophet rightly, when he foretold that there should be nothing lovely in His life and circumstances, as men count loveliness; "no form or comeliness;" "no beauty that we should desire him"?

And the same paradox, which ruled the foundation of the Church, extended also to its building up. The great statesmen, the powerful captains, in the kingdom of God were fishermen and tentmakers. Never was this characteristic incongruity of the Gospel more signally manifested than in the preaching of St. Paul at Athens. Have we ever realized the force of that single word with which the historian describes the impression left on the Apostle's mind by this far-famed city? Gazing on the most sublime and beautiful creations of Greek art, the masterpieces of Phidias and Praxiteles, he has no eye for their beauty or their sublimity. He pierces through the veil of the material and transitory, and behind this semblance of grace and glory the true nature of things reveals itself. To him this chief centre of human culture and intelligence, this—

> "Eye of Greece, mother of arts
> And eloquence,"

appears only as καζείδωλος, overrun with idols, beset with phantoms which mislead, and vanities which corrupt. Art and culture are God's own gifts, legitimate embellishments of life, even of worship, which is the highest form of life. But if culture aims at displacing religion, if art seeks to dethrone God, — why, then, in the highest interests of humanity, be it our prayer that the sword of the barbarian and the axe of the iconoclast may descend once more, and sweep them ruthlessly away. There was, at least, this redeeming feature in ancient art, that it gave expression to whatsoever sense of the Divine lay buried in the heathen mind. But art and culture, which studiously ignore God—what can be said for these? In this one word καζείδωλος lies the germ of that fierce and protracted struggle of Christianity with Paganism, which ended indeed in a splendid victory, though not without inflicting many a wound on humanity of which the scars and seams still remain. Notwithstanding the merciless scoffs of a Celsus and the biting sarcasm of a Julian—the Apostle's words were verified in their literal truth. Strength was made perfect in weakness. God chose the foolish things of the world to confound the wise, aye, and the uncomely things of the world to confound the beautiful. The things which are not, brought to nought the things which are.

So then in its accompaniments, not less than in its main idea, this incident at Bethel is a type of the Gospel of Christ. This exile, the representative of the Israel after the flesh, prefigures a greater outcast and wanderer, the representative of the Israel after the spirit, the representative of the whole family of man. This ladder reared up from earth to heaven, whereby angels ascend and descend, what is it but the Incarnation of the Eternal Word, wherein God is made man, and man is taken up into God? This it is which establishes the title of Christianity as the absolute and final religion of the world—this indissoluble union of the human with the divine—this one only adequate response to the deepest religious cravings of mankind. Hence the Church has ever clung with a tenacity of grasp, which shallow hearts could ill understand, to this central idea, the indefeasible wedlock of heaven and earth in the God-man. And to those whose sight is purged by faith, to those who are gifted with the eye of the Spirit, the vision of Bethel will be vouchsafed with a far more exceeding glory: "Verily, verily, I say unto you, Hereafter ye shall see heaven open and the angels of God ascending and descending upon the Son of Man:" on the Son of Man: yes, and on thyself too, O man, for thou art one with this Son of Man, one with the Father in Him.

"Gifted with the eye of the Spirit," I say; for in vain the heavens are riven asunder, and the glory streams forth, and all things are flooded with light, if the capacity of vision be absent.

Only the cold bare stones beneath, only the midnight gloom overhead, only the dreary, monotonous waste around, these and these alone are visible otherwise. We have been saddened, perhaps we have been disconcerted, as recently we read the dreary epitaph which sums up the creed of a brilliant man of science not long since deceased—a hopeless, soul-less, lifeless creed, to which his own very faculties and acquisitions appear to us to give the lie. We have been saddened justly; but why should we be disconcerted? God be thanked, the most absolute childlike faith has not unfrequently been found united with the highest scientific intellect. We in this place have never yet lacked bright examples of such a union, and God grant we never may. But what right have we to expect it as a matter of course? What claim do the most brilliant mathematical faculties, or the keenest scholarly instincts, give to a man to speak with authority on the things of the Spirit? Are we not told on authority before which we bow that a special faculty is needed for this special knowledge; that "eye hath not seen and ear hath not heard"; that only the Spirit of God—the Spirit which He vouchsafes to His sons—knoweth the things of God? And does not all analogy enforce the truth of this lesson? One man has a keenly sensitive musical ear, but he is colour-blind. Another has a quick eye for the faintest gradations of colour, but he cannot distinguish one note of music from another. Does the imperfect eye of the one know any haze of uncertainty over the hues of the rainbow; or the obtuse ear of the other disparage the master works of a Handel, or a Mozart, or a Beethoven? *Here* is a mathematician who sees in a sublime creation of imaginative genius only a tissue of unproven hypotheses; and *here* is a poet, to whom the plainest processes of algebra, and the simplest problems in geometry, are mere barbarian gabble, conveying no distinct impression to the brain, and leaving no intelligible idea on the mind. Judge no man in this matter. To his own master he stands or falls. But judge yourselves. Yes, spare no rigour and relax no vigilance when the judge is the criminal also. Believe it, this spiritual faculty is an infinitely subtle and delicate mechanism. You cannot trifle with it, cannot roughly handle it, cannot neglect it and suffer it to rust from disuse, without infinite peril to yourselves. Nothing—not the highest intellectual gains—can compensate you for its injury or its loss. The private prayer mechanically repeated, then hurried over, then intermitted, and at last dropped; the devotional reading found to be daily more irksome, because suffered to be daily more listless; the valuable moral and spiritual discipline of the early morning chapel, gradually neglected; the unobtrusive opportunities of witnessing for Christ by deeds of kindness and words of wisdom suffered to slip by,—these, and such as these, are the unfailing indications of spiritual decline; till disuse is followed by paralysis, and paralysis ends in death; and you are left without God in the world. And yet when again—you young men—when again, in the years to come, can you hope that the conditions of your life will be as favourable to this spiritual self-discipline as they are now? Where else do you expect to find in the same degree the opportunities for private meditation and retirement, the daily common prayer and the frequent communions, the inspiring and sanctifying friendships, the wholesome occupation for the mind and the healthy recreations for the body, every appliance and every aid which, if you will employ them aright, neither disusing them nor misusing them, will combine to build up and to perfect the man of God? Choose ye, this day. To you, more especially, I appeal who have recently commenced your residence here, and to whom, therefore, with the changed conditions of life a heightened ideal of life also is suggested. This is the momentous alternative. Shall your life hereafter be typified by the barren rocks and the monotonous waste, hard and dreary, if nothing worse; or shall it be illumined within and around with the effulgence of God's own presence, so that—

> "The earth and every common sight
> To you shall seem
> Apparelled in celestial light,
> The glory and the freshness of a dream"?

A dream? nay, not a dream, but an everlasting reality, eternal, as God's own being is eternal.

There are two ways of looking on the relations between the things of this life and the things of eternity. A false and a true. The false way regards the one as the rejection of the other. They are reciprocally exclusive. The avocations, the interests, the amusements of daily life—nature and history, poetry and art—these are so many hindrances to the heavenly life. Every moment given to work is a moment subtracted from prayer—thus the inward life becomes a constant reflection upon the conditions of the outward. This is the spirit which of old peopled the desert with anchorites; the spirit which in all ages, though under divers forms, has made a religion of selfishness. This is the voice which cries, "Lo, here! and lo, there!" though all the while the kingdom of heaven is within us, in the very midst of us. The true conception is the reverse of all this. Its ideal is not a separation, but an identification of the two. It takes its stand on the old maxim *laborare est orare.* It strives that its work shall be prayer, and its prayer shall be work. Nature and history to it are not the veil of God's presence; they are the investiture of God's glory. And, therefore, to it is vouchsafed the vision of grace, and comfort, and strength, as to the patriarchs of old. The solitary wanderer along the dreary thoroughfare of this life lays himself down. He has nothing but the bare stones beneath for a couch, and nothing but the midnight sky overhead for a tent. He closes his eyes for a moment; and the whole place is flooded with glory. Ah! the Lord was in this place, though he knew it not; but he knows it now — knows it in the access of strength, knows it in the promise of hope, knows it in the celestial voice and the ineffable light. All the common interests of life—the associations, the amusements, the cares, the hopes, the friendships, the conflicts—all are invested with a dignity and an awe unsuspected before. Reverence is henceforth the ruling spirit of his life. This monotonous round of commonplace toils and commonplace pleasures is none other than the House of God. This barren, stony thoroughfare of life is the very portal of heaven.

To read these hieroglyphics traced on nature, on history, on the human soul—to decipher this handwriting of God wheresoever it appears, and where does it not appear?—is the ultimate and final study of man. All history is a parable of God's dealings; and we must learn the interpretation of the parable. All nature is a sacrament of God's being and attributes, and we must strive to pierce through the outward sign to the inward meaning. To realize God's presence, to hear God's voice, to see God's visage,—let this be henceforth the aim and the discipline of our lives. So at length we shall pass from Bethel to Peniel —from the palace courts to the presence chamber itself. We shall see God face to face. It is a vision of power, of majesty, of awe unspeakable; but it is a vision also of purification, of light, of strength, of life. The blessing is won at length by that long lonely wrestling under the midnight sky. The fraud, the worldliness, the self-seeking is thrown off like a slough. All is changed. Old things have passed away. The supplanted rises from the struggle, the supplanter rises no more, but the Israel, the Prince, who has power with God and with men. Shall not Moses' prayer then be our prayer, "Lord, I beseech Thee, show me Thy glory"?

"Show me Thy glory." Where else shall this glory reveal itself if not in the studies of this place? These properties of numbers, these selections of space, these phenomena of light, of heat, of energy, of life, of language, of thought, what are they? Individual facts to be recorded, arranged, tabulated, marshalled under several heads, which we call laws, and having so called them, with a strange self-complacency and contentment fold our hands, as if nothing more were to be done, as if by the mere imposition of a name we had crowned them absolute sovereigns of the Universe? Or are they manifestations—partial, indeed, and needing to be supplemented—of a power, a majesty, a wisdom, an order, a beneficence, a finality, a oneness, a One, who is shown to us as the Eternal Father in the revelation of the Eternal Son? Can we afford to look down from the serene heights of modern science and culture on the untutored Indian, who saw God's face in the shifting clouds, and heard God's voice in the whistling winds? Nay, was there not a truth in this childish ignorance which threatens to elude the grasp of our manhood's wisdom? Was it altogether a baseless dream in those stoic Pantheists, who endowed each several planet with an animating spirit of its own? altogether a wild fancy in those Christian fathers assigning to each its particular angel, who should whirl it through space and hold it in its course? Was it not rather a Divine instinct feeling after a higher truth? Human life cannot rest satisfied with the science of phenomena alone. It needs to supplement science with poetry. And the true, the absolute, the final poetry is the recognition of God the Creator and Governor, of God the all-wise and all-powerful, of God the Father, the Redeemer, the Sanctifier, of God the eternal love. "Blessed are they who have eyes to see,"—thus to them

> "The meanest flower that blows can give
> Thoughts that do often lie too deep for tears."

Thoughts of immortality, of wisdom, of light, of love.

"Show me Thy Glory," where else again shall His glory be seen, if not in those friendships which are the crowning gift of University life? This intimate communion of soul with soul, this linking of heart with heart, is it merely a matter of human convenience, of human preference, or has it a Divine side also? This love, this devotion, this reliance of the weak on the strong, this reverence for a nature purer, nobler, more upright, more manly, more unselfish than your own—what is its meaning? It is a precious, unspeakably precious, gift of God, you will say —far beyond wealth, or fame, or popularity, or ease, or any earthly boon of which you can conceive. Yes, but it is more than this. May we not call it in some sense a sacrament, a sign and a parable of your relation to your Lord?

You are awed—no other word will express this feeling—you are awed with the honour done to you by this friendship. You do not talk much about it—it is too sacred a thing—but you do feel it. You confess to yourself day and night your own unworthiness. And yet, though you strive to be worthy, you would not wish to feel worthy. The very sense of undeservedness invests the gift with a bountifulness and a glory which you would not forego. The fountains of your thanksgiving would cease to flow freely if you claimed it as a right; and it is a joyful and a pleasant thing to be thankful. Apply this experience to the infinitely higher gift of Christ's friendship, of Christ's sacrifice. Herein lies the power of the Cross—which men called and still call weakness—the power which awes, inspires, energises, which elevates the heart and sanctifies the life—herein this feeling of boundless thanksgiving arises from this sense of absolute undeservedness. For is it not true, that those will love most to whom most is given and forgiven? So then this your friendship is found to be none other than the House of God. The Lord is in this place, and happy are ye if ye know it.

Once again; look into your own soul, and what do you find there? Yes, ye yourselves are the temple of the living God. He is there—there, whether you will or not. Through your reason, through your conscience, through your remorses and regrets, through your capacity of amendment, through your aspirations and ideals, He speaks to you. You are His coinage. His image and superscription are stamped upon you. Aye, and He has also re-stamped you, re-created you, in Christ Jesus by the earnest of His Spirit. If it be true of your body that it is fearfully and wonderfully made, is it not far more true of your soul? Henceforward you will regard yourself with awe and reverence, as a sanctuary of the eternal goodness. You will not, you dare not, profane this sanctuary. Here is the true self-respect — nay, not self-respect, for self is abased, self is overawed, self veils the face and falls prostrate in the presence of Infinite Wisdom, and Purity, and Love thus revealed. Surely, surely the Lord was in this place—in this poor, self-seeking, restless, rebellious soul of mine, and *I*, I thought it a common thing, I went on my way heedless, I followed my own devices and desires, I knew it not.

In conclusion, I have been asked to plead before you to-day a cause which it should not require many words of mine to enforce. The Barnwell and Chesterton Clergy Fund appeals to you year by year for aid. Of all claims this (I say it advisedly) should be a first charge on the liberality of members of the University.

These populous and growing suburbs are created by your needs. They are chiefly peopled by college servants and others for whom you are responsible. Zealous clergy are willing to work for the work's sake in these districts commonly for stipends which no one could call remunerative—sometimes for no stipends at all. And yet it is still the same old story which I remember years ago. There is still the same difficulty in meeting current expenses; still the same fear lest the spiritual machinery should be impaired for lack of funds; still the same precarious hand-to-mouth existence, of which we heard complaint in years past. Is it quite creditable that matters should go on thus? In a thousand ways you all, some directly, some indirectly, you all are reaping, materially, intellectually, or spiritually the fruits gathered from the liberality of past ages? Will you not make an adequate return? Steady, continuous subscriptions are needed. A liberal response to this day's appeal is needed. The Fund is largely dependent on the proceeds of the University Sermon. Not less than a hundred pounds will suffice to meet all requirements. Will you not give it this day, either in this church, or in contributions sent afterwards to the treasurer? Think not that you hear only the poor words of the preacher in this appeal. Christ Himself pleads with you. Christ's own words ring in your ears, "Ye did it, ye did it not, to *Me*." Ah, yes, the Lord was in this place—in this weary pleading of the preacher, in these trite commonplaces of spiritual need: and *we*, we knew it not. God grant that you may know it in time. God forbid that He should ever say to you, "I knew you not."

THE CONSCIOUSNESS OF SIN HEAVEN'S PATHWAY.*

"When Simon Peter saw it, he fell down at Jesus' knees, saying, Depart from me; for I am a sinful man, O Lord."—LUKE v. 8.

To those who search the Scriptures, not because in them they think they have eternal life, but because in them they trust to find historical difficulties, this account of St. Peter's call has seemed to reward their search. The narrative indeed, is simple and inartificial in itself; the incidents follow in a natural order; the traits of character are wonderfully realistic and lifelike. There is confessedly an air of truthfulness about the whole story; but how—how, it is asked—can this account be reconciled with the narrative given in St. John's Gospel? There we have a wholly different story of St. Peter's call. His

* Preached in St. Paul's Cathedral on Sunday Afternoon, September 6th, 1874.

brother Andrew is a scholar of the Baptist. The Baptist points out Jesus to Andrew and to a fellow-disciple. They follow Jesus; they are accepted by Him; they lodge that day with Him; they are convinced that He is the Christ. Andrew takes his brother Simon to Jesus; Jesus receives him. "Thou art Simon, the son of Jona. Thou shalt be called Cephas." This account also is perfectly plain, but how can the two be harmonised? "Have we not here," it is said, "two irreconcilable narratives—in fact, two distinct legends of the call of St. Peter?"

I have more than once remarked that the apparent moral contradictions of the Bible are often its most valuable moral lessons. A similar remark will apply to its apparent historical contradictions. Underlying these is very frequently a subtle harmony, which eluded us at our first hasty search. The two accounts are after all not contradictory, but supplementary, the one to the other. So it is here. Read St. Luke's narrative carefully, and it will be apparent that this cannot have been the first meeting of St. Peter with our Lord. I say nothing of the healing of his wife's mother, for, though this is related earlier in St. Luke's Gospel, yet it is plain from the narrative in the other evangelists that it is not related here in chronological order.

But what are the facts? These fishermen have

been toiling throughout the night; their labour has been wholly unrewarded, though night is the proper season for plying their craft; and now in the bright glare of the morning sun—now when, after the ill-success of the night, it would be perfect madness to expect a haul—now they are suddenly, imperiously bidden to put out again into the deep sea, and to let down their nets. And the command is obeyed. There is the lurking misgiving, there is the tacit remonstrance; but there is prompt obedience notwithstanding. "Master, we have toiled all the night; nevertheless, at Thy word I will let down the net." "*At Thy word.*" Who is this, that this most unreasonable demand meets with such ready acquiescence? Is it possible that He can have been a mere passing stranger, or a mere casual acquaintance? How could His advice have been entertained for a moment when He told an experienced fisherman to do what a fisherman knew to be utterly foolish and futile? The narrative itself, I say, implies some previous knowledge of our Lord on St. Peter's part. He would never have acted as he is represented here as acting unless he had believed, or, at least, had suspected, that there was a more than human power and intelligence in our Lord. In short, the narrative of St. Luke presupposes the narrative of St. John. Jesus speaks to Peter now as one who has a right to command. The incident in St. John gives the personal call of Peter; the incident in St. Luke gives his official call. On the one occasion he is represented as a disciple and a follower; on the other occasion he is declared an apostle and a teacher. "From henceforth thou shalt catch men."

But I did not select this text with any special purpose of discussing historical difficulties. Such discussions, indeed, are necessary when they are forced upon us, but they only distract the mind from the moral and spiritual lessons of the Scripture. Nor, I think, is the lesson in · the text difficult to extricate. All history teaches by example, and the Scriptural narrative is the intensification of history. The miracles of our Lord are not miracles only. They are most frequently acted parables also. And have we not here a parable of the most intense pathos and of the widest application?

"Master, we have toiled all the night, and we have taken nothing." What is this but a true, painfully true, image of the efforts, the struggles, the futilities, the despairs of humanity; not in isolated cases, here and there only, of disappointed hopes and unrealised aim, but with thousands of men and women who are born into this world, and live and labour, and suffer and die, without securing any substantial and enduring good, simply because they have lived and died apart from God, who alone survives the decay of time, and alone can give satisfaction to the immortal spirit of man?

"We have toiled all the night." Yes; we see it now—now when the morning light of eternity has burst upon our aching eyeballs. We have toiled all the night. There was darkness above and around us; there was toil of hands and toil of heart; there was the struggle for subsistence; there was the race after wealth and honour; there was the eager pursuit of phantom goods. We had our pleasures and we had our pains. We had our failures and we had our successes. Yes, our splendid successes as men counted them —as we were half tempted to count them ourselves. But we have taken nothing. Our successes are as our failures; our pains are as our pleasures, now. In the all-absorbing abyss of time we have taken nothing, absolutely nothing —nothing which can escape the jaws of the grave, nothing which will pass the portals of death. We stand alone, stripped of everything, alone with God, alone with eternity.

You pursued wealth, and you pursued it not in vain; you determined that your career should be a success, and a success you made it. You surrounded yourself with every material comfort; you added to these substantial appliances all the embellishments and all the refinements of life. What then? Did they give you the satisfaction you hoped for? Could you feel that there was any finality in such aims and acquisitions as these? No. The hope was better after all than the realisation; the prospect was brighter than the attainment. You were restless, discontented, craving still. There was a hunger of soul, though you would not confess it—a hunger of soul, which rejected and loathed these husks. And now where are they, and what are they? Or you pursued honour and fame, and men lavishly bestowed upon you that which you so eagerly sought, till you seemed at length to have all, and more than all, that you had set your heart upon. But still there was no contentment, because there was no finality. Dropsy-like your craving only grew with the gratification. Each fresh draught of applause created a fresh thirst. Every imagined slight, every unintentional neglect, every trivial rebuff, was a keen agony to you. You had only increased your sensitiveness; you had not secured your satisfaction. Or, again, you had set your heart on human love, God's greatest boon if you use it without misusing it, if you subordinate it to his Divine love. Your human affections, your human friendships, were everything to you. In the buoyant hopefulness of youth, in the solid security of middle age, it seemed as though these must last for ever. But soon enough the painful truth dawned upon you. The march of life began to tell on your comrades in the journey. One dropped at your side, and then another. The ranks were visibly thinning, and there was no one to step in and take the vacant places. First the mother at whose knees you had lisped your earliest faltering prayer; then the friend who shared all your counsels, who was more than a brother to you; then the wife whom you cherished as another self; then the little daughter whose innocent childish talk had solaced you in many a grievous hour: so, one by one, they fell away, and you are left gradually alone and more alone; they leave you when you need them most, and at length in the vacancy of your solitude you make the bitter discovery that though you have toiled all night you have taken nothing—you have taken nothing at all.

A short time ago we laid in the vaults of this cathedral the last mortal remains of one [*] who has achieved for himself a foremost place among the masters of his art in our own age. It was fit that his bones should lie here, side by side with more than one famous brother sculptor who has gone before him—side by side with the most illustrious names in the sister art of painting; with Reynolds, whose easy grace in the delineation

[*] Mr. Foley, R.A., sculptor.

of human portraiture stands quite without a rival; with Turner, who has succeeded as no other painter has succeeded, in any age or country, in reproducing on canvas the subtle play of light and shade, the ever-varying aspect, the depth, the infinity, of external nature; with Landseer, too, our most recent guest in this our artists' resting-place, whose genial and vigorous representations of the lower animal life have invested it with almost a human interest, and, so doing, have taught us many a suggestive lesson of humanity and kindliness. Side by side, too, with England's greatest architects, and Wren, their prince, whose genius needs no word of eulogy here, for his monument is above and around us. Such a place of sepulture well befitted such a man. It is our tribute of respect for noble gifts nobly used. It is our expression of thanksgiving to God, who thus endows His servants that they may employ their endowments to exalt and to embellish human life.

But one thought cannot fail to strike us here. We may remember that the great conqueror of modern time, when it was suggested to him to perpetuate some signal incident in his triumphant career by an historical picture, asked how long the work would last. He was told two or three centuries—perhaps, under favourable circumstances, five centuries. This would not satisfy his devouring ambition. This was not the immortality of fame which he had designed for himself. He must have a more enduring memorial than this. Compared with the canvas of the painter, the marble of the sculptor is long-lived indeed. The most enduring of human works are the works of the sculptor's chisel. The stern granite features of the Pharaoh who befriended Joseph and the Pharaoh who persecuted Israel may still look down on the land which they ruled with an iron rule between three and four thousand years ago. The winged lions and winged bulls on which the contemporaries of Shalmanezer and Sennacherib may have gazed in awe, in the royal palaces of Assyria, still confront us in our national museum with the same weird look, unchanged though all else has changed, surviving still, though a hundred generations of men have been born, and lived, and died, meanwhile. And it may be that in the centuries to come, some curious explorer will exhume, from the grass-grown mounds of this ruined city, a work of art bearing the name of him whom on Friday last we bore to an honoured resting-place—perhaps the effigy of a prince who flourished in a remote epoch of the past, when England was still a nation, and who sank into an untimely grave amidst a people's mourning. And thus the sculptor's fame will have a second lease of life.

But after all, thirty centuries are but as three—are but as three years or three days—compared with eternity. Napoleon's ambition was a perverted instinct, but it was an instinct, nevertheless. Man feels that he was not made to die; he will not consent to die. This thirst for enduring fame, what is it but an echo, a mocking echo, of an eternal verity? Yes, he will live. The materialist may tell him that, when the eye and the ear are dissolved into gases and decomposed into dust, it matters nothing to him with what honours men may adorn his memory, with what praises they may celebrate his name. He, too—his personality, or what he was pleased to call his personality—is dissolved, is dissipated, is gone; but the materialist never yet has been able, never will be able, to persuade mankind. The natural instinct of man revolts against the assumption; and the ambition of the Christian, the ambition for eternity alone, expresses truly this general instinct of man. To labour for the good things of this world, to labour for fame in the coming centuries, what is it, after all, if our views are bounded by this narrow horizon? Why, then, like the disappointed fishermen of the Galilean lake, we have toiled all the night long, and, for our pains, we have taken nothing.

And this change—this conversion, if you will—comes sometimes, it may be, despite ourselves, but comes—remember this—comes most often in answer to some act of obedience, to some surrender of self-will on our part. We may complain; we may demur; we may distrust. We have toiled all the night, and have taken nothing; but we recognise the authority of the Divine voice, and we force ourselves into compliance —" nevertheless, at Thy word." The command is general: it has come to all alike,— " Let ye down your nets." But, like Peter, we specialise it, we adopt it, we appropriate it to ourselves : " I will let down the net." And so we do what seems hard and unreasonable; we do what we have never done before.

And the response—the response to this obedience—is a light flashed in upon our soul, a double revelation, a revelation of mixed pleasure and pain, for it is a revelation at once of the sin within and of God without. The marvellous bounty of God's grace dazzles and astounds our vision, and, in our perplexity of heart, the despairing, craving, forbidding, yearning cry is wrung from our lips, " Depart from me ! Depart from me, O Lord, for I am a sinful man !"

" Depart from me, O Lord." I know it all now. I see my sin, because I see Thy goodness. Yes, I have beheld Thy holiness, Thy purity, Thy truth, Thy grace, Thy love, and I have been stunned with the contrast to self. The brightness of the light has intensified the blackness of the shade. Depart from me, O Lord! what can I have in common with Thee?—I, so selfish, so vile, so sin-laden, with Thee, so merciful, so righteous, so holy. In very deed, Thy ways are not as my ways, and Thy thoughts are not as my thoughts. Depart from me, O Lord! This "fear of the Lord" is, indeed, the "beginning of wisdom." This consciousness of sin is the true pathway to heaven. The saintliest of men have ever felt and spoken most strongly of their own sinfulness. The intensity of their language has provoked the sneer of the worldling—has been an evidence here of their own conviction that, despite their pretensions to holiness, they are no better than he, perhaps somewhat worse. But they know, and he doth not know, what sin means and what God means, and so the despairing cry is wrung from their agony, "Depart from me, O Lord."

"Depart from me, O Lord! And yet not so, Lord." Even while Peter is speaking his gestures belie his words. His lips implore Jesus despairingly to depart, but his eyes and his hands entreat Him passionately to stay. "Not so, Lord, for how can I endure to part with Thee? In Thy presence is hope, is light, is joy. Lord, to whom shall we go? Thou hast the words of eternal life. Depart from me? No; it is for the godless to say, 'Depart from

us, for we desire not the knowledge of God.'
It is for the unclean spirits to rave against
Thee—' Let us alone, Thou Jesus of Nazareth!
What have we to do with Thee?' But I, I have
everything to do with Thee. I am created in the
image of God. I have a ray of the Divine light,
a seed of the Divine word, within me. And like
seeks like; therefore I yearn after Thee, therefore
I am drawn towards Thee, therefore I stretch out
my hands to Thee over the wide chasm of sin
which yawns between us. Depart from me?
Nay, rather abide with me. Teach me, absolve
me, purify me, strengthen me. Take me to
Thyself, that I may be Thine and Thine only.
Abide with me, for the day of this life is far
spent, and the night cometh when no man can
work. Stay with me now and evermore, and so
fulfil Thy gracious promise: 'If a man love Me
and will keep My word, My Father will love him,
and we will come unto him, and make our abode
with him.'"

THE HISTORY OF ISRAEL
AN ARGUMENT IN FAVOUR OF CHRISTIANITY.*
" They are Thy people and Thine inheritance."—DEUT. ix. 29.

IT is related of a certain royal chaplain that,
being asked often by his sovereign to give a

* Sermon preached in St. Paul's Cathedral on Sunday, May 21st, 1876.

concise and convincing argument in favour of Christianity, he replied in two words—"The Jews." It is this subject which I offer for your consideration this afternoon—the history and character of the Israelite race as a witness to Christianity. The subject is certainly not inappropriate at this season, when the commemoration of the great Pentecostal Day is fast approaching, to which all the previous history of the nation had tended, which substituted the dispensation of the Spirit for the dispensation of the Law, and expanded the religion of a tribe into the religion of mankind. It is, moreover, forced upon our notice by that remarkable chapter in Deuteronomy which we have heard this afternoon, and which, by prophetic insight, brings out with singular distinctness the prominent character and subsequent career of the race. Only reflect upon such expressions as these:—"Go in to possess nations greater and mightier than thyself, cities great and fenced up to heaven"; "Understand, therefore, this day that the Lord thy God is He which goeth over before thee"; "The Lord thy God giveth thee not this good land to possess it for thy righteousness; for thou art a stiffnecked people"; "Ye have been rebellious against the Lord from the day that I knew you."

Read these passages in the full light which

thirty centuries of the nation's history have thrown upon them. Study this contrast between their character and their achievements as it unfolds itself in all their subsequent history. Consider, on the one hand, not only the first conquest of Canaan to which the words more immediately refer, but the succession of far more brilliant victories over the great nations of the world, culminating in that most magnificent triumph of all — the triumph of Christianity. Consider, on the other hand, not only those early murmurings and idolatries in the wilderness to which the language more directly points, but that long catalogue of rebellions of which the subsequent history of Israel is made up, and which reached its climax in the martyrdom of the Lord of Life. Set these one against the other, and you will confess that the utterances of Deuteronomy are wonderful anticipations of the future, succinct epitomes of centuries yet to come. You may question, if you will, every single prophecy in the Old Testament, but the whole history of the Jews is one continuous prophecy, more distinct and articulate than all. You may deny if you will every successive miracle which is recorded therein, but again the history of the Jews is, from first to last, one stupendous miracle, more wonderful and convincing than all. *Here* you have a, small, insignificant people—stiff-necked, rebellious, worthless ; *there* you have the most magnificent spiritual achievements—the most signal moral victories. What conclusion can you draw, except that which is drawn for you in the words which I have read: " The Lord thy God is He that goeth before you"?—"They are Thy people and Thine inheritance, which Thou broughtest out by Thy mighty power and Thy stretched out arm."

Look first at the capacities of the people themselves. They had no remarkable gifts which might have led us to anticipate this unique destiny. They had no intellectual qualities of a very high order like the Greeks—vivid imagination, subtlety of thought, æsthetic taste; no political capacity like the Romans, no organizing power or faculty of legislation which might secure for them the ascendency over the nations of the world. They were, moreover, a stubborn, exclusive, intolerant people—an unpractical people, without the power, or at least the will, to adapt themselves to the institutions, the feelings, and the prejudices of the people with whom they were brought in contact. They were believed, in consequence, to cherish an universal hatred against the rest of mankind ; and they, in turn, were hated by all—hated, not with the hatred of an admiring envy, but the hatred of a supercilious scorn. Of all the tribes on the face of the earth the Jews, we should have said, were the very last to ingratiate themselves with the other races of mankind, and to lay the civilised world at their feet. And now turn from the people themselves to the land of their abode. Certainly this does not enable us to solve the enigma. Palestine does not occupy a large space in the Christian's imagination; for it is a very minute, insignificant spot in the map of the world. It is, moreover, incapable of expansion, for it is bounded on all sides either by sea or mountain ranges, or by vast and impracticable deserts. To a great extent all this country is mountainous and barren, and even this meagre and unpromising territory is not all their own. The sea-coast would have been valuable to a people gifted with commercial instincts. With commerce they might have extended their influence; but from the sea-coast they were wholly excluded. The Phœnicians on the north and the Philistines on the south occupied all the most important harbours; and this territory of the Jews was so unexpansive, so barren, so unpromising that they were placed at a still greater disadvantage when compared with the surrounding people. The Jews are surrounded on all sides, and by the most formidable neighbours. On the one side by Egypt, a country of the highest fertility, the foremost military power in the world, with an ancient civilisation which dated from a period long before the birth of the father of the Israelite people, whilst it stood foremost of the human race in works of art in its day. Who was Israel, then, that he could withstand Egypt? There, again, on the other side, was another mighty empire, first Assyria, then Babylon, the only rival of Egypt of the ancient world. In these places they had the same advantage of wide plains of exceptional fertility, a high and remote civilisation, an army of tremendous strength, and a centralisation under an absolute rule, with all the resources which a great and vast dominion could command. As Persia succeeded Babylon, and as Babylon succeeded Assyria, so Persia—far more mighty and terrible—overruns and conquers all Western Asia. Egypt itself falls. Palestine is a mere speck, surrounded by the huge dominions of the Persian monarch. What chance has Israel against such terrible neighbours? Must it not be crushed and ground to atoms and annihilated by its foes? But, at all events, it might have been supposed that, however stubborn and impracticable they were in their attitude towards others, they would at least be united amongst themselves—that they would be loyal to their country, that they would be faithful to their laws and institutions, that they would be true to their God. This internal cohesion would give them strength to resist—this absolute harmony would win for them an influence that would compensate for the superior advantages of their more powerful neighbours. But what do we find as a matter of fact? Their national history is one continuous record of murmuring, of rebellion, of internal feuds, of moral and spiritual defection. They have no sooner escaped from their Egyptian bondage, their necks still bearing the scars of the tyrants' yoke, than they fall into shameless idolatry. The worship of the golden calf is only the type and presence of still more guilty lapses in centuries yet to come; the revolt against Moses and Aaron only the type and shadow of the rebellious spirit to which Israel rose in the distant future. Again and again the religion of Jehovah is effaced, or almost effaced, from the mind of the nation. Again and again the hideous idolatries of Moloch—idolatries cruel, profligate, and shameless—supplant the worship of the Lord of heaven and earth. And the political condition of the nation is not one whit more hopeful than the religious. When unity alone can save the people then there is disruption. The Ten Tribes are severed from the House of David, never to be united again. The power of one kingdom is spent in neutralising the power of the other. This is a concise history of the race during the period from the disruption to the captivity. The career of Israel, from first to last, is a running comment upon the words, "Not for thy righteousness or for the uprightness of thine heart dost thou go to possess the land," for "ye have been rebellious against the Lord from the day that I knew you." Not once or twice only the Mighty Archer has strung His weapon and pointed His shaft, and His aim has been frustrated by Israel's disobedience. His chosen instruments have been snapped in His hands, starting aside like a broken bow. Indeed, the history of Israel is quite unique in the chronicles of nations. The chronicles of other nations record the qualities as well as the crimes of the people whose career they commemorate. They praise their patriotism, their prowess, their manifold virtues, their magnificent achievements. But the Bible, the chronicle of the Jews, is one uninterrupted catalogue of sins and shortcomings—one long bill of indictment against Israel. One only is true, one only is faithful, one only is victorious; for he fears not the nation, but the nation's God. So then, however we look at the matter, there is nothing which affords ground for hope; and when we question actual facts, we find they correspond altogether to those expectations we should have formed beforehand from the character and position of the nation. Never has any people lived upon the earth who passed through such terrible disasters as the Jews. Never has any people been so near to absolute extinction again and again, and yet have survived. Again and again the vision of the prophet has been realised. Again and again the valley of the shadow of death has been strewn with the dry bones of carcases seemingly extinct. Again and again there have been seasons of dark despair, when even the most hopeful, challenged by the Divine voice, could only respond, " O Lord God, Thou knowest!" But again and again there has been a shaking of the dry bones—the bones have come together, bone to bone; they have been strung with sinews and clothed with flesh; breath has been breathed into them, and they have lived, and have become an exceeding great army. Think of those many centuries of Egyptian bondage, when the life of the nation seemed to have been strangled in its infancy. Reflect next on that period in its youthful career, when it is fighting its way inch by inch, and struggling for very existence in Palestine, doing battle with nations greater and mightier than itself, and with " cities fenced high up to heaven." Look forward again, and we see its fate during the manhood of the nation under its king, the land now divided against itself and overrun by successive invaders. As of old so now again, but in a far more terrible sense, Israel finds himself face to face with the Anakims and with those great empires of the East before whom he appears but as a grasshopper. The end was inevitable. For a time Israel was a plaything in the hands of those terrible neighbours, tossed to and fro between two powerful rivals—Egypt on the one side, and Assyria and Babylon on the other—till at length, in a moment of victory, he is swept away, and his place knows him no more. Could anything seem more hopeless than the revival of the nation from the Babylonish captivity? Yet from Babylon, as from Egypt, Israel returned. A new lease of life was granted, and with it there followed a new lease of disaster also. His old fate pursued him still. The saying was fulfilled which had been spoken by the prophet: "That which the locust hath left hath the canker-worm eaten, and that which the canker-worm hath left hath the caterpillar eaten." He was rescued from the fangs of Babylon only to be food for the Assyrians. He was drawn from the feet of the Assyrians only to be devoured by the insatiable Roman. And yet all the while—and this is the remarkable fact to which I ask your attention—amidst calamities the most overwhelming and suffering the most intense—exiled, enslaved, trampled under foot, only not annihilated—all the while he was hopeful, was jubilant, was triumphant still. He was always dying, and behold he lived. Century after century prophets had declared, in no ambiguous terms, that despite all these adverse appearances, despite all these wearisome delays, Israel had a magnificent future. The nations might rage, and the kings of the earth might do their worst—they were powerless against Israel's destiny. A sceptre should rise out of Jacob which would subdue the world, and a King should sit on David's throne before whose footstool all the nations of the earth should bow A standard should be set up in Zion around which all mankind should rally. "Behold thou shalt call a nation that thou knowest not, and nations that knew not thee shall run unto thee because of the Lord thy God, and for the Holy One of Israel ; for he hath glorified thee ; " " The sons of them that afflicted thee shall come bending unto thee, and all they that despised thee shall bow themselves at the soles of thy feet ; " " Enlarge the place of thy tent, and let them stretch forth the curtains of thine habitation ; spare not, lengthen thy cords, and strengthen thy stakes ; for thou shalt break forth on the right hand and on the left, and thy seed shall inherit the Gentiles, and make the desolated cities to be inhabited."

And these hopes—these extravagant hopes—were more than realized. A King *did* rise out of Jacob to whom all the nations of the civilised world have rendered homage such as no sovereign received before or after—the homage of their heart, the homage of their lives. At the call of Israel the Gentiles flocked to the standard set up in Zion. From far and near, the cultivated Greek, the proud Roman, Assyrian and Egyptian, master and slave, are flocking around that standard. From east to west, from the ancient civilisation of India to the barbarous islands of the Pacific, Israel has dictated its sentiments, its belief, its morals, its laws and institutions to the nations. An influence far deeper, far wider, far more tenacious has appeared from that despised, insulted, down-trodden people than was ever achieved by the splendid literature of Greece or the historic empire of Rome. These are not theories, but facts—facts which some will attempt to explain away, but facts which none can deny. *Here* is the prophecy—*there* is the fulfilment. The prophecy is not a single isolated prediction of ambiguous meaning, but large and clear, written across the whole history of a nation from margin to margin. And the fulfilment corresponds to the prophecy; it is legible to all men, because stamped on the face of the world. Is there not here the manifestation of Divine providence? Do we not rightly claim the Jews as the principal witnesses to Christianity, or shall we set all this down as mere accident, a freak of fortune, a superficial correspondence without any essential connection? Shall it be regarded as mere accident that, within a few years after the appearing of this King who has thus gathered the Gentiles to His standard, Jerusalem is destroyed, and the nation scattered to the four winds of the earth—that the polity of Israel for ever ceased, that the Temple shook, and that revival was rendered thenceforward impossible? Shall we say that it is mere argument that for eighteen centuries—a period as long as that which elapsed from the proclamation of the law by Moses to the fulfilment of the law by Christ—this state of things has remained? Or should we not rather say that in this coincidence also there is a Divine significance—that He proclaimed with no uncertain sound the obituary of the old order and the commencement of the new—that God's seal is stamped upon the character of the Church, whereby Israel after the Spirit is substituted for Israel after the flesh? Do we ask what it was which gave the Jewish people this toughness, this vitality, this power? The answer simply is, "They are Thy people and Thine inheritance, which Thou broughtest out by Thy mighty power, and by Thy stretched out arm." It was the consciousness of this close relationship with Jehovah, the omnipotent and ever-present God—it was the sense of their glorious destiny, which marked them out as the teachers of mankind. It was the conviction that they were the possessors of glorious truths, and that those truths must in the end prevail, whatever present appearances might suggest—this was the secret source of their strength, notwithstanding all their faults, and despite all their disasters. Do we ask again how it came to pass that, when Israel called to the Gentiles, the Gentiles responded to the call and flocked to its standard? Here, again, the answer is simple—"Because of the Lord thy God, and for the Holy One of Israel." The Gentiles had everything else in their possession, but this one thing they lacked—knowledge of God, their Father; and without this all their magnificent gifts could not satisfy—could not save them. Therefore, when at length the cry went forth, "Ho! every one that thirsteth, come ye to the waters," they hurried to the fountains of salvation to slake their burning thirst. Culture and civilisation, arts and commerce, institutions and laws,—no nation can afford to undervalue these; but not only do all these things soon fade, but the people themselves fall into corruption and decay if the Breath of Life be wanting.

And as with nations, so with individuals. We may cultivate the intellect to the highest pitch;

we may surround ourselves with all the luxuries and refinements of civilisation; we may accumulate all the appliances which make life enjoyable; but the time will come when these things will fail to sustain us. It may come in some season of bereavement, in the hour of sickness or of loss. It may come in the failure and decay of powers. It may come in the pains of our death-agony. It may come—and this is the most solemn thought of all—after we have passed the confines of the grave. But come it must sooner or later; for we are children of God, and we cannot with impunity ignore or deny the Father of earth and heaven. There only is rest and peace; there only is true life for the soul of man.

THE VISION OF GOD.*

"And they shall see His face."—REV. xxii. 4.

IT is related of the greatest of the Bishops of Durham that, in his last solemn moments, when the veil of the flesh was even now parting asunder, and the everlasting sanctuary opening before his eyes, he "expressed it as an awful thing to appear before the Moral Governor of the world."

* Sermon preached in Durham Cathedral on the Occasion of his Enthronement, on Thursday, May 15th, 1879.

The same thought, which thus accompanied him in his passage to eternity, had dominated his life in time—this consciousness of an Eternal Presence, this sense of a Supreme Righteousness, this conviction of a Divine Order, shaping, guiding, disposing all the intricate vicissitudes of circumstance and all the little lives of men—enshrouded now in a dark atmosphere of mystery, revealing itself only in glimpses through the rolling clouds of material existence, dimly discerned by the dull and partial vision of finite man, questioned, doubted, denied by many, yet visible enough now to the eye of faith, working patiently but working surely, vindicating itself ever and again in the long results of time, but awaiting its complete and final vindication in the absolute issues of eternity—the truth of all truths, the reality of all realities, the one stubborn steadfast fact, unchangeable while all else is changing—this Presence, this Order, this Righteousness—in the language of Holy Scripture, this Word of the Lord which shall outlive the solid earth under foot, and the starry vault overhead. "They shall perish, but Thou remainest, and they all shall wax old as doth a garment; and as a vesture shalt Thou fold them, and they shall be changed; but Thou art the same, and Thy years shall not fail." "All flesh is as grass, and all the glory of man as the flower of grass. The grass withereth, and the flower thereof falleth away—but the word of the Lord endureth for ever."

It is no arbitrary conjecture that this was the dominating idea of Butler's life. Early and late it is alike prominent in his writings. In the preface to his first great work, his volume of sermons, he speaks of "the Author and Cause of all things, who is more intimately present to us than anything else can be, and with whom we have a nearer and more constant intercourse than we have with any creature." In his latest work, his Charge to the Clergy of Durham, he urges the "yielding ourselves up to the full influence of the Divine Presence:" he bids his hearers "endeavour to raise up in the hearts" of their people "such a sense of God as shall be an habitual, ready principle of reverence, love, gratitude, hope, trust, resignation, and obedience;" he recommends the practice of such devotional exercises as "would be a recollection that we are in the Divine Presence, and contribute to our being in the fear of the Lord all the day long." Thus his death-bed utterance was the proper sequel to his life-long thoughts. The same awe-inspiring, soul-subduing, purifying, sanctifying Presence rose before him as hitherto. But the awe, the solemnity, was intensified now, when the vision of God by faith might at any moment give place to the vision of God by sight. Not unfitly did one, writing shortly after his decease, compare him to "the bright lamps before the shrine," the clear, steady light of the sanctuary, burning night and day before the Eternal Presence.

In the strength of this belief he had lived, and in the awe of this thought he now died. This conviction it was—this sense of a present righteousness, confronting him always — which raised him high above the level of his age; keeping him pure amid the surroundings of a dissolute court; modest and humble in a generation of much pretentious display; high-minded and careless of wealth in a time of gross venality and corruption; firm in the faith amidst a society cankered by scepticism; devout and reverent, where spiritual indifference reigned supreme; candid and thoughtful and temperate, amidst the temptations and the excitements of religious controversy; careful even for the externals of worship, where such care was vilified as the badge of a degrading superstition. Hence that tremendous seriousness which is his special characteristic — that "awful sense of religion," that "sacred horror at men's frivolity," in the language of a living essayist. Hence that transparent sincerity of character, which never fails him. Hence that "meekness of wisdom," which he especially urges his clergy to study, and of which he himself was all unconsciously the brightest example.

And what more seasonable prayer can you offer for him who addresses you now, at this the most momentous crisis of his life, than that he—the latest successor of Butler—may enter upon the duties of his high and responsible office in the same spirit; that the realisation of this great idea, the realisation of this great fact, may be the constant effort of his life; that glimpses of the invisible righteousness, of the invisible grace, of the invisible glory, may be vouchsafed to him; and that the Eternal Presence, thus haunting him night and day, may rebuke, may deter, may guide, may strengthen, may comfort, may illume, may consecrate and subdue the feeble and wayward impulses of his own heart to God's holy will and purpose!

And not for the preacher only, but for the hearers also, let the same prayer ascend to the throne of heaven. In all the manifold trials and all the mean vexations of life, this presence will be your strength and your stay. Whatsoever is truthful, whatsoever is real, whatsoever is abiding in your lives, if there be any antidote to sin, and if there be any anodyne for grief, if there be any consolation, and if there be any grace, you will find it here, and here alone—in the ever-present consciousness that you are living face to face with the Eternal God. Not by fitful gusts of religious passion, not by fervid outbursts of sentimental devotion, not by repetition of approved forms, and not by acquiescence in orthodox beliefs, but by the calm, steady, persistent concentration of the soul on this truth, by the intent fixing of the inward eye on the righteousness and the grace of the Eternal Being before Whom you stand, will you redeem your spirits and sanctify your lives. So will your minds be conformed to His mind. So will your faces reflect the brightness of His face. So will you go from strength to strength, till, life's pilgrimage ended, you appear in the eternal Zion, the celestial city, wherein is "neither sun nor moon, for the glory of God doth lighten it, and the Lamb is the light thereof."

Let this, then, be the theme of our meditation this morning. Many thoughts will crowd upon our minds and struggle for utterance on a day like this; but we will put them all aside. Not our hopes, not our cares, not our burdens; nothing of joy, nothing of sadness shall interpose now to shut out or obscure the glory of the Presence before Whom we stand.

Not our hopes, though one hope starts up and shapes itself perforce before our eyes. It will be the prayer of many hearts to-day that the inauguration of a new Episcopate may be marked by the creation of a new See; that Northumberland, which in the centuries long past gave to Durham her Bishopric, may receive from Durham her due in return in these latest days; that the Newcastle on the Tyne may take its place with the Old Castle on the Wear, as a spiritual 'fortress strong in the warfare of God.

Not our cares, though at this season one anxiety will press heavily on the minds of all. The dense cloud, which for weeks past has darkened the social atmosphere of these northern counties, still hangs sullenly overhead. God grant that the rift which already we seem to discern may widen, till the flooding sunlight scatters the darkness, and a lasting harmony is restored to the relations between the employer and the employed.

Not our burdens, though on one at least in this Cathedral the sense of a new responsibility must press to-day with a heavy hand. If indeed this burden had been self-sought or self-imposed, if his thoughts were suffered to dwell on himself and his own incapacity, he might well sink under its crushing weight. But your prayer for him, and his ideal for himself, will shape itself in the words which were spoken to the great Israelite restorer of old, "Not by might, nor by power, but by My Spirit, saith the Lord of Hosts."

In this strength only, before you as before him, will the great mountain become a plain.

Therefore we will lay down now our hopes and our fears, our every burden, at the steps of the altar, that, entering disencumbered into the inmost sanctuary, we may fall before the Eternal Presence.

The vision of God is threefold—the vision of Righteousness, the vision of Grace, the vision of Glory.

I. The vision of Righteousness is first in the sequence. Righteousness includes all those attributes which make up the idea of the Supreme Ruler of the universe—perfect justice, perfect truth, perfect purity, perfect moral harmony in all its aspects. Here, then, is the force of Butler's dying words. Ask yourselves, Can it be otherwise than "an awful thing to appear before the Moral Governor of the world"? You have read, perhaps, the written record of some pure and saintly life, and you are overwhelmed with shame as you look inward and contrast your sullied heart and your self-seeking aims with his innocency and cleanness of heart. You are confronted—you, an avowedly religious person—in your business affairs with an upright man of the world; and his straightforward honesty is felt by you as a keen reproach to your disingenuousness and evasion, all the keener because he makes no profession of religion. Yes, you know it; this is the very impress of God's attribute on his soul, though God's name may seldom or never pass his lips. And if these faint rays of the Eternal Light, thus caught and reflected on the blurred mirrors of human hearts and human lives, so sting and pain the organs of your moral vision, what must it not be, then, when you shall stand face to face before the ineffable Righteousness, and see Him in His unclouded glory!

It is a vision indeed of awe, transcending all thought; a vision of awe, but a vision also of purification, of renewal, of energy, of power, of life. Therefore enter into his presence now and cast yourself down before His throne. Therefore dare to ascend into the holy mountain; dare to speak with God amidst the thunders and the lightnings; dare to look upon the face of His righteousness, that, descending from the heights, you, like the lawgiver of old, may carry with you the reflection of His brightness, to illumine and to vivify the common associations and the every-day affairs of life.

Not a few here will doubtless remember how an eloquent living preacher in a striking image employs the distant view of the towers of your own Durham—of my own Durham—seen from the neighbourhood of the busy northern capital only in the clearer atmosphere of Sundays—as an emblem of these glimpses of the Eternal Presence, these intervals of Sabbatical repose and contemplation, when the furnaces and pits cease for the time to pour forth their lurid smoke, and in the unclouded sky the towers of the celestial Zion reveal themselves to the eye of faith. Let this local image give point to our thoughts to-day. "Unto Thee lift I up mine eyes, O Thou that dwellest in the heavens. Behold, even as the eyes of servants look unto the hand of their masters, and as the eyes of a maiden unto the hand of her mistress, even so our eyes wait upon the Lord our God."

II. But the vision of Righteousness is succeeded by the vision of Grace. When Butler in his dying moments had expressed his awe at appearing face to face before the Moral Governor of the world, his chaplain, we are told, spoke to him of "the blood which cleanseth from all sin." "Ah, this is comfortable," he replied; and with these words on his lips he gave up his soul to God. The sequence is a necessary sequence. He only has access to the Eternal Love who has stood face to face with the Eternal Righteousness. He only who has learned to feel the awe will be taught to know the grace. The righteous Judge, the Moral Governor of the World, is a loving Father also, is your Father and mine.

This is the central lesson of Christianity. Of this He has given us absolute assurance, in the life, the death, the words, and the works of Christ. The incarnation of the Son is the mirror of the Father's love. What witness need we more? Happy he who shall realise this fact in all its significance and fulness. Happy he on whom the light of the glory of the Gospel of Christ, who is the image of God, shall shine, he who shall—

> "Gaze one moment on the Face Whose beauty
>   Wakes the world's great hymn;
> Feel it one unutterable moment,
>   Bent in love o'er him;
> In that look feel heaven, earth, men, and angels,
>   Distant grow, and dim;
> In that look feel heaven, earth, men, and angels,
>   Nearer grow through Him."

Yes, it is so indeed. All our interests in life, the highest and the lowest alike, abandoned, merged, forgotten in God's love, will come back to us with a distinctness, an intensity, a force, unknown and unsuspected before. Each several outline and each particular hue will stand out in the light of His grace. Thus we are bidden to lose our souls only that we may find them again; we are charged to give up houses, and brethren, and sisters, and father, and mother, and wife, and children, and lands—all that is lovely and precious in our eyes—to give up all to God, only that we may receive them back from Him a hundredfold, even now in this present time. Our affections, our friendships, our hopes, our business and our pleasure, our intellectual pursuits and our artistic tastes—all our cherished opportunities and all our fondest aims must be brought into the sanctuary and bathed in the glory of His Presence, that we may take them to us again, baptized and regenerate, purer, higher, more real, more abiding far than before.

III. And thus the vision of love melts into the vision of glory. So we reach the third and final stage in our progress. This is the crowning promise of the Apocalyptic vision, "They shall see His face." The vision is only inchoate now; we catch only glimpses at rare intervals, revealed in the lives of God's saints and heroes, revealed above all in the record of the written Word and in the Incarnation of the Divine Son. But then no veil of the flesh shall dim the vision; no imperfection of the mirror shall blur the image; for we shall see Him face to face—shall see Him as He is—the perfect truth, the perfect righteousness, the perfect purity, the perfect love, the perfect light. And we shall gaze with unblenching eye, and our visage shall be changed. Not now with transient gleams of radiance, as on the lawgiver of old, shall the light be reflected from us; but resting upon us with its own ineffable glory, the awful effluence—

> " Shall flood our being round, and take our lives
> Into itself."

Of this final goal of our aspirations—of this crowning mystery of our being—the mind is helpless to conceive, and the tongue refuses to tell. Silent contemplation, and wondering awe, and fervent thanksgiving alone befit the theme. Even the inspired lips of an Apostle are hushed before it. "Beloved, now are we the sons of God, and it doth not yet appear what we shall be; but we know that, when He shall appear, we shall be like Him, for we shall see Him as He is"—we shall see Him as He is.

THE HEAVENLY TEACHER.*

"He shall take of Mine, and shall show it unto you."— ST. JOHN xvi. 15.

THE death of Christ was the orphanhood of the disciples. I am not inventing a figure of my own when I say this. It is the language which our Lord Himself uses to describe their destitute condition. In our English Bible He is made to speak of leaving them comfortless. The words in the original are: "Leave you orphans"—

* Preached in St. Peter's Church, Bishop Auckland.

"Leave you desolate," as it is translated in the Revised Version. They would be fatherless, motherless, homeless, friendless—at least, so it seemed to them—when He was gone.

No condition of life excites so keenly the compassion of the compassionate as the helplessness of the orphan. It is not only that a child is deprived, by its parents' death, of the means of subsistence; its natural guardian, teacher, friend is gone. Henceforth it is a waif on the ocean of the world. In no respect different was that void which threatened the disciples when the Master's presence had been withdrawn. They had left all —authority, home. They had forsaken parents and friends, and He had become Father and Mother, and Sister and Brother to them. They had given up houses and land, and He was henceforth their home. Their dependence on Him was absolute. Whatever of joy they had in the present, and what of hope they had for the future, were alike centred in Him. They thought His thoughts and lived His life. And now this communion of soul with soul, and of life with life, must be ruthlessly severed.

This was the terrible shock for which Christ would prepare the minds of His disciples. It was not only the void of earthly hopes scattered by His death; but their Teacher, their Guide, Spirit, Friend, Christ, their Father was withdrawn.

The voice which soothed must be silent, and the eye which gladdened must be glazed, and the hand which blessed must be stiffened in death. Christ lay buried—lost for ever, as it would seem to them. What joy, what strength, what comfort could they have henceforth in life? They would stake their whole on Christ, and Christ has failed them. Surely, never was orphanhood more helpless, more hopeless, than the orphanhood of these poor Galileans.

It was to prepare them for this terrible trial that the promise in the text was given. He must go; but another shall come. They should not be without a teacher, a guide; one Advocate, one Comforter would be withdrawn, but another would take His place. There would be a friend still, an adviser ever near to take them by the hand, to whisper into their ears, to prepare, to instruct, to protect, to fortify, to guide them into all truth. Another comforter. Yes; and yet not another. There would not be less of Christ, but more of Christ, when Christ was gone. This is the spiritual paradox which is assured to the disciples by the promise in the text—" He shall take of Mine, and show it unto you. All things that the Father hath are Mine; therefore, said I, He shall take of Mine and shall show it unto you." Another, and yet not another. It was not Christ supplanted, not Christ superseded, not Christ eclipsed and quenched, but a larger, higher, purer, more abundant Christ with whom henceforth they should live. It was not now a Christ who might be speaking at one moment and the next moment might be hushed, but a Christ whose tongue was ever articulate and ever audible—Christ vocal even in His very silence. It was not now a Christ who was seen at one moment, and the next was concealed from view by some infinite obstacle, but a Christ whose visit no darkness could hide and whose touch no distance could detain. It was not a Christ of now and then, not a Christ of here and there, but a Christ of every moment and every place—a Christ as permeating as the Spirit is permeating. "He shall take of Mine, and shall show it unto you." "Lo, I am with you alway! I am with you even to the end of the world."

He is not lost, then. This is the promise which Christ gives to His disciples on the eve of His departure to console them for their loss. His departure was more than necessary. It was even expedient, it was even advantageous for them that He should go. Did not the Saviour say this? Nothing would have seemed more improbable in the anticipation than that the death of Christ should have produced the effect it did produce on His disciples. We should have predicted weakness, depression, misery, scepticism, apostacy, despair; and yet what was the actual result? Why, all at once they appear before us as changed men. All at once they shake off meaner hopes; all at once their nerves are fortified, are lifted into a higher region. On the eve of the catastrophe they are hesitating, fearful, sense-bound, narrow in their ideas. They are, we might almost say, "of the earth earthy." And on the morrow they are strong, steadfast, courageous, endowed with a new spiritual faculty which bears unto the very salvation of salvation. Hitherto they have known Christ after the flesh. Henceforth they will know Him so no more.

To know Christ after the flesh! What would we not have given to have known Him after the flesh? What a source of strength it would have been to us, we imagine, just to have listened to one of those parables spoken by His own lips; just to have witnessed one of those miracles of healing wrought by His own hand; just to have looked one moment on Him as He stood silent in the judgment-hall, or bleeding on the cross! But no! It was expedient for us, as it was expedient for the first disciples, that He should go away. It was expedient for us; otherwise the Spirit could not come.

To know Christ after the flesh! Did not the disciples know Him after the flesh, and did they not forsake Him? Did not Thomas who doubted and Peter who denied know Him after the flesh? Did not the Jewish mob which hooted and reviled, and the Roman soldiers who scourged, know Him after the flesh? What security was this knowledge after the flesh against scepticism, against blasphemy, against apostacy, against rebellion? Seeing, it is said, is believing. Yes, and hearing, too. But it is the seeing of the spiritual eye and the hearing of the spiritual ear—the eye that beheld the heavens open and the Son of Man standing on the right hand of God: the hearing of the glory when He was called into Paradise, "unspeakable words which it is not lawful for a man to utter."

To know Christ after the flesh. Why should we desire to know Him after the flesh? It was just to unteach the disciples themselves, whose knowledge was only after the flesh, that Christ went away, because so long as they were possessed of this knowledge, the Paraclete could not come, could not take up His abode in their faith. Thus, this is the work of the Spirit, as described by our Lord, in the text to us, as to the disciples of old. The Spirit offers not less of Christ, but more of Christ; for in the place of the Christ who walked on the shores of the Galilean lake, who sat on the brink of the Samaritan well, and shed tears over the doomed city—instead of such a Christ we have a Christ who is ever present to us; a Christ of all times and all places; a Christ who traverses the universe—an Omnipotent Christ.

Look at the explanation which our Lord Himself gave to the prophets: " He shall take of Mine, and shall show it unto you." How so? Why of Christ, and Christ only? Has the Spirit nothing else to teach us? Hear what follows: " All things—*all things*—that the Father hath are Mine; therefore, said I unto you, He shall take of mine and shall show it unto you."

All things! Yes; all history, all science, all aggregation of truth in whatever domain, and whatever kind it may be. "Think you," He seems to say—"think you that My working is confined to a few paltry miracles wrought in Galilee? The universe itself is My miracle. Think you My words are restricted to a few short precepts uttered to the Jews?" We make foolish distinctions. We imagine we erect a barrier within which we would confine the Christ of our own imagination; but the Christ of Christ's own teaching overleaps all such barriers of ours. We are careful to distinguish between knowledge and revealed religion. We separate Christ from the former and we relegate Him to the latter; but the Christ of Christ's own teaching is the Eternal Word, through whom the Father speaks.

We draw the rigid lines of demarcation between science and theology, between religion and language, but the Christ of the people is the hand of the Father not less in science and language than in religion and theology. We have our distinctions between the secular and the spiritual, as if the two were antagonistic. We must not use a saying of Christ, as if it taught that our duty to Cæsar was something quite apart from our duty to God; as if, forsooth, it were possible for us to have any moral obligation to any man, or body of men, to any child, which was not also an obligation to God in Christ. But the Christ of the Gospel claims sovereignty over all alike—over that which we call secular not less than that which we call spiritual. "All things—*all things* —that the Father hath are Mine; therefore, I say, He shall take of Mine, and show it unto you."

We speak sometimes of the revelations. Yes; revelations, indeed, not merely of inanimate processes, not merely of blind laws, but revelations of the eternal world, of the Eternal Son through whom the Father works. Therefore, as Christians, we are bound to look upon these as Christ. Therefore, if we are true to our heavenly schooling, the Spirit will take up these and show them unto us. "He shall take of Mine, and shall shew it unto you."

Are we diligent students of the lessons of history? Do we delight to trace the progress of the human race from the first dawn of civilisation to its noonday blaze? To disclose the obscure past of the great nations of the earth? to mark the development of the arts of government? to follow the ever-widening range of intellect? to discern the stream of human life broadening slowly down with the force of ages?

Then let us see the kingdom of Christ not less in the progress of history than in the laws of science. He was in the world, and the world knew Him not. He was the true Light that lighteth every man — the Light ever brighter and clearer till it attained its full glory at length in the Incarnation. Therefore the school of history is also the school of the Holy Spirit, for it is the setting forth of Christ. "He that hath eyes to see, let him see." "He shall take of Mine."

If you have traced Christ's footprints in the processes of Nature; if you have heard Christ's voice in the teachings of history—then, surely, you will not fail to see and hear Him in your own domestic and social relations. That pure affection which has been to you a fountain of benediction; that friendship which has been the crowning glory of your life—can you think of it apart from Christ? If you do not find Christ here, assuredly you will seek Him in vain elsewhere. What was that truthfulness, that purity, that unselfishness, that devotion which attracted you to the broken light of the Great Light, a reflected ray from the Central Sun Himself? Yes, the Spirit took of Christ and showed it to you when, through that affection, through that friendship, He held up to you the nobler, because a more God-like, idea of life. " He shall take of Mine." He shall bring all things to your remembrance, whatsoever I have said to you.

Last and chiefest, for the crown of all these—these rays through forest and mountain—of all other lessons, He shall set before you the full Sun. He shall teach you the lesson of Incarnation. He shall show unto your soul the tremendous importance of that statement which comes from your lips as time after time you repeat your creed : " He was made man." He shall teach you the lesson of the Passion. He shall remind you day and night of the paramount obligation which it lays upon you. Think—yes, think and think, and think—of that word till the love of Christ shall constrain your whole being, shall bind you hand and foot, and lead you captive to the will of God. He shall teach you the lesson of the resurrection, emancipating, purifying, strengthening, exalting, till he makes you conformable thereunto. Then you will rise from the sepulchre in which you have lain many days, will breathe the pure air of God's presence once more, will sit at meat when you are risen ; while, though in the world, you will be no longer of the world ; notwithstanding all disabilities and weaknesses you will live—live even now as faithful citizens of the kingdom of heaven, which is righteousness, and peace, and joy in the Holy Ghost.

NOTE.—These Sermons are printed from reports.

CHRISTIANITY AND PAGANISM.*

I.

IN the lectures which I addressed to you this last year, I took as my subject the early history of Christianity while it was still unrecognised by Roman law, and, therefore, treated as an enemy of the State. On this occasion I purpose to trace the stream a little further from its source, when Christianity has forced itself into recognition and become the predominant religion of the empire. The struggle between Christianity and Paganism has entirely changed its outward character. The only weapons which the Church could wield at a former epoch were moral and spiritual. She is now furnished with all the appliances of political and social prestige; yet these, however imposing, and to some extent serviceable, are not her really effective arms. She can afford to be deprived of them for a time, and her career of victory is unchecked. Her

* Delivered at St. Paul's Cathedral, Tuesday evening, November 4th, 1873.

substantial triumphs must still be won by the old weapons. The source of her superiority over Paganism is still the same as before—a more enlightened faith in the will of the unseen, a heartier devotion to the cause of humanity, a more reverential awe for the majesty of purity, a greater readiness to do and to suffer. The change has been as startling and as sudden as it was momentous. All at once the Church had passed from hopeless, helpless oppression to supremacy and power. For several years after the opening of the fourth century the last and fiercest persecution still raged. Christians were hunted down, tortured, put to death with impunity and without mercy. The only limit to their sufferings was the weariness or the caprice of their persecutors. Yet before the first quarter of this century has drawn to a close the greatest sovereign who had worn the imperial diadem for three hundred years is found presiding at a council of Christian bishops discussing the most important questions of Christian doctrine as though the fate of the empire depended upon the result. In the short period of fifteen years which elapsed between the death of Galerius and the Council of Nicæa, the most stupendous revolution which the pages of history record had been brought about. We cannot wonder that the contemporary heathen failed altogether to recognise its completeness and its permanence. Even to ourselves, who look back at the struggle between Christianity and Paganism from the vantage ground of history, it is difficult to realise the suddenness of the transition. To those who lived in the heat of the conflict, and whose estimate of relative proportions was necessarily confused by the nearness of this position, it was altogether unintelligible. The one thing which most astonishes us in heathen writers at this period is their blindness to the real significance of the change. They ignore it, or they make light of it; they speak of Christian sects, of Christian offices and Christian rites, in a tone of cold indifference where they think fit to mention them at all. Obviously they look at Christianity as a phenomenon which it may be curious to contemplate, but which has no great practical moment for them; they do not realise it as destined to mingle permanently with the main stream of human life. Christianity to them is still a mere Syrian superstition which has become the fashion of the day, as so many other superstitions have been before it, and, like its predecessors, will pass away when it has had its fling. The truth is, that the revolution was not really sudden, though it seemed so. In its social and political aspects, its victory was almost instantaneous, but essentially it was a moral revolution; and such revolutions are ever gradual: they provoke no notice because they are noiseless; they advance patiently and silently, step by step; and then only when the work is done do indifferent spectators discover that any work has been going on. Their true type is that temple of God in whose building neither hammer, nor axe, nor tool of iron was heard, because the stones had been brought thither ready hewn for the building.

In this course of lectures it is my design to discuss the fall of Paganism and the triumph of Christianity in the Roman empire; but obviously this subject is too large for adequate treatment within the space of three short lectures. I am obliged, therefore, to limit it in some way or other; and it seemed to me that I could not do better than take the reign of Julian the Apostate as the central feature in the picture, and group around it such other facts as may be required to explain its significance. There are many advantages in this mode of treatment. This Paganism was never exhibited to more advantage than in the person of this, its greatest and most energetic champion. High personal character, no common intellectual gift, great military renown, supreme political power, perfect knowledge of his adversary, absolute and unflinching devotion to his own cause —all these united to make Julian the most formidable antagonist which the Church ever had, or might be expected to have. His career showed what Paganism could do, and what it could not do. The ability of the champion only exposed the helplessness of the cause. And again, a full blaze of light is poured upon this one man and this one reign such as rarely falls to any period of ancient history. Julian himself, devoted friends, impartial critics, sworn foes, heathen and Christian, orthodox and Arian—all have contributed to the completeness of the portraiture. This strange character, half philosopher, half fanatic, the most wary of dissemblers, and the most Quixotic of adventurers, stands before us with a distinctness of feature which leaves nothing to be desired.

In order to understand the man and the epoch it is necessary to take up the course of history more than half a century before he ascended the throne. The starting-point in our review of events is the most remote province of the empire—the island of Britain. On the 25th of July, 306, Constantine was proclaimed Emperor by the Roman Legionaries at York. " Oh, happy Britain," says a heathen panegyrist, not then foreseeing the stupendous results, " Oh, happy Britain! that it has first seen Constantine as Cæsar." This was the commencement of a long reign, extending over more than thirty years—the longest in the annals of Imperial Rome since Augustus. In the interval of three centuries which separated these two remarkable men, no emperor had reigned who deserved to be considered great as they were. And their lives are linked together in another way. The one reign saw Christianity cradled in the manger; the other witnessed it seated on the throne. On October 27th, 312, some two miles from the walls of Rome, where the Great North Road crosses the Tiber, was fought the decisive battle of the Milvian Bridge. The routed army with its captain and rival Emperor, the heathen champion Maxentius, perished in the waters of the Tiber, and Constantine entered the Imperial city—the stronghold of Paganism—in triumph. On June 15th, 313, was signed the great charter of religious toleration—the Edict of Milan, issued in the joint names of the Emperors Constantine and Licinius. By this edict Christianity was recognised as a lawful religion. The sacred places, and the property which had been taken from the Christians during the great persecution were restored to them once more. Every man was allowed henceforth to adopt any form of worship which he might choose. On the 25th of July, 325, the anniversary of his accession and the inauguration of the twentieth year of his reign, Constantine, then sole Emperor, brought the Council of Nicæa to a close. He had been present at several of its sittings, and throughout had exerted himself to the utmost to secure unanimity. By a higher inspiration, yet not without his instrumentality, the deliberations of the assembled Bishops resulted in the Creed which was to be henceforth and for ever the basis of unity in the Church.

But, meanwhile, what was Constantine himself? It is strange that, notwithstanding the prominent part taken by this Emperor in the establishment and consolidation of the Church, historians have been found to doubt the genuineness of his conversion. I do not think that the facts justify any such hesitation. For the sincerity of his Christian profession we have two guarantees, which, combined, must, I think, be regarded as conclusive. It was gradual, and it was disinterested. It was gradual. I shall say nothing here of his miraculous conversion, of the fiery cross in the heavens, with the inscribed words, " Hereby conquer," which is said to have appeared to him shortly before the battle of the Milvian Bridge. What truth underlies this story we shall never know ; but, judging by his public actions, we trace a gradual advance towards a more distinct reception of Christianity. His father Constantine had been a believer in one God. He had extended his protection to the Christians when they were persecuted by his Imperial colleagues. This Monotheism and this toleration descended to Constantine, as it were, by inheritance. For some years after his accession he appears not to have advanced much beyond this point. On the triumphal arch erected in Rome to commemorate his victory over Maxentius, and which still spans one of the approaches of the Forum, his success is ascribed to the suggestions of "the Divinity." Such language is exactly what his father, who was not a Christian, might have used, what heathen philosophers did use again and again. This vague expression, "The Divinity," is repeated several times afterwards in Imperial edicts. There is as yet no personal profession of Christianity. The Edict of Milan puts the Christians on the same political level as the Pagan. It gives them no advantage; but, by degrees, his language becomes more explicit, and his legislation more directly favours the Christians. The Council of Nicæa is the climax of aggressive ascent. Again it was disinterested. As a mere question of worldly policy, I think it can hardly be doubted that Constantine acted very unwisely in embracing Christianity. His Christian subjects were still a comparatively small minority—an aggressive minority it is true, but not a dangerous minority if properly handled. They would have been won over to a man by frank toleration as they had been won over to his predecessor, Alexander Severus, and to his father, Constantius Chlorus. They asked nothing more than this. But by the further step of declaring himself a Christian he had nothing to gain and very much to lose. He alienated the heathen subjects, while his Christian subjects were devoted to him already. Indeed, as a matter of fact, it is quite plain that his conversion did lead to much disaffection, and that he was greatly hampered by it. Take an instance of this. The secular games, the great festival of thanksgiving for the prosperity of Rome, recurred, according to Roman usage, at long intervals of about one hundred and ten years. They were celebrated with great pomp and magnificence, and accompanied by elaborate propitiatory sacrifices to the tutelary deities of Rome. They had been kept last under Severus, and the time had come for another celebration. But year after year of the long reign of Constantine passed, and no notice was taken of them. No omission would have wounded more deeply the sensibilities of the Romans than this. The heathen historian Zosimus, writing a whole century after, ascribed all the woes that had befallen the empire to this one fatal neglect. Again, during his second and last visit to Rome, the Capitoline games were celebrated. A main feature in the ceremonial was a procession along the sacred way to the Temple of Jupiter on the Capitol, in which the Emperor himself was expected to take a part. He flatly refused. Looking down from his residence on the Palatine Hill as the magnificent train wound round its foot, he broke out into expressions of ridicule and contempt. The senate and people were mortally offended. On one occasion, probably during this very visit, his statues were pelted with stones. This insult was reported to Constantine by some indignant courtier. The Emperor passed his hand across his brow. He had a strong sense of humour. "Strange," said he, "that I did not feel hurt." But he did feel hurt, nevertheless; hurt in dignity by this insolence of the Romans, and a new capital arose on the shores of the Bosphorus in protest against the outrage. Christian Constantinople was his revenge on heathen Rome. "He made himself a Greek," said Dante, "to leave Rome to the Pope." Doubtless the Papal power grew more freely when the shadow of the Imperial presence was removed; but the Pope was not in Constantine's mind, and the immediate effect was a deadly side-thrust at heathendom. Rome, the stronghold of heathen sentiment and worship, languished rapidly from this time. Paganism had been stabbed in the heart.

But while the sincerity of Constantine cannot reasonably be doubted, his inconsistency is quite beyond question. The fact is that he was half a Pagan to the end, and, as Niebuhr has truly said, we do him a grievous wrong if we judge his actions by a purely Christian standard. In this respect he was only like many of his contemporaries. In that age of transition the best heathens were half Christians, and not the best Christians were half heathens. The semi-Paganism of Constantine is matched by the semi-Christianity of Julian. I am not concerned with the moral inconsistencies of this Emperor. The sins of

Constantine will not condemn the truth of Christianity, any more than the virtues of Julian will re-instate the errors of Paganism. Constantine is allowed on all hands to have been temperate in his habits and chaste in his life; but the domestic history of this great Sovereign was darkened by one horrible tragedy. About twelve months after the Council of Nicæa, in which he had borne so conspicuous a part, the Roman world was horrified by the report of three murders in the Imperial household. The Emperor's eldest and favourite son, Crispus—a young man of highest promise—an idol of the public; his little nephew—a bright, engaging boy of twelve; his own wife, Fausta, the mother of his three younger sons, were ruthlessly put to death. What was the secret of this tragedy we shall never know. It seems most probable that the son was implicated in some dangerous conspiracy, that the nephew was an unconscious tool of the conspirators, and that the wife, having goaded the husband in the first flush of his anger to extreme measures against her stepson, herself fell a victim to the violence of his remorse when the revulsion came. There were, we may safely say, circumstances which might extenuate these horrible crimes; there could be none which could justify them. A dark, indelible stain rests on the memory of Constantine.

But if the moral inconsistency of Constantine is the more shocking, his religious inconsistency is the more bewildering. In his recently built capital he erected a statue of himself, which exhibited a strange medley of the old and the new, and which may well serve for a type of his career as a sovereign. The Emperor was represented as a follower of the Deity, whom he himself had adopted as his patron in the old days of his Paganism—the Deity whom his apostate nephew ever regarded with special reverence; but in the aureole which encircled the head the rays took the form of the nails, the instruments of Christ's passion. It was believed that at the base of this statue Constantine had placed a fragment of the true cross. It is also stated that in this same place was deposited the palladium—the cherished relic of Pagan Rome, which Æneas was said to have rescued from the flames of Troy, and which Constantine himself stealthily removed to his new capital. It is just the same with his legislation. Thus we find almost side by side, promulgated within two months of each other, two Imperial decrees—the one enjoining that Sunday shall be set apart as a day of rest; the other providing that when the palace or any public building is struck by lightning, the soothsayers shall be consulted as to the meaning of the prodigy, according to ancient custom, and the answer reported to the Emperor himself. When, indeed, we see this juxtaposition of Christianity and Paganism, we are forcibly reminded that Constantine was one and at the same time the summoner of the Nicene Council and the chief Pontiff of heathenism. Thus, at one moment, he was preaching sermons to his courtiers and discussing dogmas with his bishops; and, at the next, he was issuing orders for the regulation of some Pagan ritual. The same fountain *did* send forth sweet waters and bitter. And this incongruity held him captive to the last, even beyond the gates of death. In his newly built eastern capital—Christian Constantinople—he was buried by his own directions in a church amidst the memorials of the apostles, and "the equal of the apostles" was the title accorded to him by common consent. In his forsaken western capital—heathen Rome—he was, as a matter of course, deified, as his Imperial predecessors had been deified, as he himself had deified his own father Constantius; and by virtue of this apotheosis he took his rank, not only with an Augustus or a Trajan, but with a Commodus and a Caracalla among the gods of Olympus. A strange blending of incongruous elements. And yet, whatever may have been felt of Constantine's life, however much of Paganism may have alloyed his Christianity hitherto, when the end came there was no more halting between two opinions. Failing health to one who was endowed with a singularly robust constitution came as an unmistakable sign of the approaching change. The warning was not lost upon him. The increased fervour of his devotions was noticed by all. On one occasion he spent a whole night in the church praying. Strange to say, this zealous theological disputant, this foremost champion of the truth, had not hitherto been baptised. He was not even a catechumen. But now, when he felt himself sinking, he eagerly pressed that baptism might not be delayed. This wish was granted, and the rite was administered. This done, he devoutly expressed his thanksgivings for the mercy vouchsafed to him, and his readiness to go at once on his last heavenward journey. He refused again to assume the Imperial purple, and, so arrayed still in the white robe of his baptism, he was laid on his couch to await the end.

On the 22nd of May, 337—it was Whit Sunday, the appropriate festival of the newly baptised— about noon, the great Emperor breathed his last. He was succeeded by his three sons—Constantine, Constantius, and Constans. The three princes were scarcely seated on the throne, when the Imperial family became again the scene of a horrible tragedy as shocking as that which had left so dark a stain on their father's life. The soldiers rose up and massacred not less than nine princes of the blood—the brothers and nephews of the deceased Emperor. Nearly a century later an untrustworthy historian gives currency to a story that Constantine himself had directed these massacres, having discovered that he had been poisoned by his brothers. For this shameful libel on them and on him there is absolutely no foundation. All the circumstances are against it, and it may safely be dismissed as a foul calumny. More specious is the view that the new Emperor Constantius, then a young man of twenty-one, was implicated in the massacre; but it was done, if not by his direct orders, at least with his tacit connivance. But, however this may be, the incident has a very direct bearing on the subject of these lectures. In this carnage, besides the three Emperors themselves, two children alone escaped. The other members of the Imperial family perished to a man. The survivors were the two sons of one of Constantine's brothers, Julius Constantius; Gallas, a boy of twelve or thirteen; and Julian, a child of six or seven, of whom we shall hear much hereafter. Their father and their eldest brother were amongst the slain.

Of the three brothers who divided the empire of Constantine we are concerned only with one—the eldest, Constantine, and the youngest, Constans, perished in two successive revolutions. The middle and surviving brother, Constantius, united again all the dominions of his father under his sceptre. He alone left his mark on the history of the Church. He alone shaped the destinies and swayed the feelings of his relative, Julian. It is worth our while to form a closer acquaintance with this man, who was the evil genius of his cousin and ward. Constantius had not inherited the towering strength and commanding mien of his father. He was under the average height, with a long body and short, bowed legs. His complexion was very dark, his hair smooth and glossy. He had prominent and keen eyes, recalling the piercing glance which his father Constantine had cast around on the assembled Bishops in the Council-hall of Nicæa, and which never failed to strike awe into the beholders. The crimes of Constantine were those of a strong, impulsive, half-barbarous nature. The crimes of Constantius were due to cold calculation and to indifference to the commonest claims of humanity. He was cautious to excess, sparing of his rewards, and backward in his confidences. He was mean, selfish, suspicious almost to fanactism, shrinking from no cruelty when his fears were alarmed. It is noticed as characteristic of the man that when borne through the streets of Rome on a triumphal chariot he was seen, notwithstanding his short stature, to bend his head as he passed under each archway. Yet he was not a man without redeeming virtues and some real ability. Like his father, he was temperate and just, so that, notwithstanding his many enemies, scandal itself was forced into silence. He could be sparing of rest and prodigal of labour when the interests of the State demanded it. He was gracious, too, in his demeanour, and with many—as even his cousin Julian is obliged to confess—bore a reputation for clemency. He sustained the honours of his Imperial rank with a dignity which never forgot itself, while he showed a contempt of mere vulgar popularity which even unfriendly critics described as magnanimous. Of his disastrous influence on the religious sentiments of Julian I shall have to speak hereafter. For the present I confine myself to the part which he took in determining the relative positions of Christianity and Paganism in the empire. Unlike his father Constantius, he had been brought up a Christian from his infancy. His doctrinal views were very distorted, his moral conduct was often a gross libel on the Gospel; but where it was a question between Paganism and Christianity the sympathies of the Emperor were exerted wholly and undisguisedly on the side of the latter. On the whole, therefore, there is less of heathenism in the public memorials and the official acts of this reign than in the preceding. The Pagan emblems diminish; the Pagan enactments in the Statute Book are fewer. But still Constantius, like Constantine, continues to hold the office of supreme pontiff, and this necessarily leads to an official complicity in the rites and institutions of Paganism. In this capacity he issues edicts for the service of heathen sepulture, for the repairing of heathen temples, for the support of heathen priests. When, a quarter of a century later, the heathen orator Symmachus pleaded the cause of expiring Paganism before the Emperor of his day, he appealed to

6

the example of Constantius, who, though himself possessing a different faith, respected the ancient rites, and provided for their due maintenance out of the public treasury. But avarice often overleaped the bounds which the Imperial laws prescribed. The sacred name of the Gospel was again and again profaned during this reign by spoliation and violence, just as under our own Tudor Kings the cause of reformation was sullied by the selfish rapacity of the nobles. The Court of Constantius was beset with greedy and unscrupulous adventurers; and knowing the private sympathies of the Emperor, they would not be slow to seize the opportunities where any real or reported scandal of Paganism gave a handle for interference. Such opportunities would not be rare. Thus Paganism held on, still maintained and protected by law, but exposed to occasional outrages from individual violence, when, by a sudden catastrophe, it found itself seated once more on the throne.

On the 3rd of November, 361, in the twenty-fifth year of his reign, Constantius died. The event was altogether unexpected; he was still in the prime of life, only forty-five years of age. Temperate habits and vigorous outdoor exercises had kept him in perfect and unbroken health; but he was seized with a fever, and sank rapidly. There was only time to send to Antioch for the Bishop to administer that sacrament, which is ordained as the inauguration, but which, with him, as with his father, was the consummating act of his Christian profession. Immediately after his baptism he expired. His cousin Julian, the only surviving Prince of the house of Constantine, was his unquestioned successor. Thus Christianity, having wielded the Imperial sceptre for more than half a century, was again deposed. Of the education and the apostasy, of the reign and work of the new Emperor, I hope to speak to you in my two concluding lectures.

II.*

IN my lecture last Tuesday I passed under review the two long reigns of Constantine and Constantius, comprising altogether a period of fifty-five years. We were thus brought to the accession of Julian. What, then, was the change wrought in the relations of Christianity and Paganism during this period? Most persons, I imagine, would answer without misgiving that Christianity had been established on the ruins of heathenism. This answer, however, would be wholly inaccurate. Paganism was in no sense disestablished, and Christianity was only in a very limited sense established. Paganism was still the official religion of the empire. Whatever

* Delivered in St. Paul's Cathedral, Tuesday evening, November 11th, 1873.

might be the individual faith of the sovereign, yet, as the head of the State, he was still the chief representative of heathenism, both in life and in death. In life he was the supreme pontiff, the fountain head of authority over all the priests, temples, rituals, throughout the empire; in death the representation was transformed from earth to heaven. By his apotheosis he became a patron divinity of Rome. A pagan calendar is still extant in which all the festivals of the deified Constantine are duly recorded. Now there was not and there could not be any such alliance with the State on the part of Christianity. However strong might be the Emperor's personal sympathies; however much he might mix himself up in the internal affairs of the Church; whatever privileges or immunities he might extend to the clergy,—yet officially he had no recognised position, officially he was a Pagan still. When, therefore, it is said that Paganism was disestablished and Christianity established in its stead, the position of affairs is entirely misconceived. The personal religion of the sovereign had nothing whatever to do with the official religion of the State. In modern countries, for the most part, the two coincide, and it is well that this should be so; but there are some exceptions. England under James II., and Saxony at the present moment, are cases in point.

But while Paganism was in no sense disestablished, Christianity might be said to a certain extent, though only to a very limited extent, to have been established side by side with it. The principle which in our own day has been called "levelling up," had been partially adopted. Christianity was not only tolerated as a lawful religion, but some political privileges had been extended to it. Thus, for instance, one enactment of Constantine exempts the Christian clergy from certain onerous duties, while another secures to the Pagan priests this same privilege. In this respect the two religions are put on exactly the same footing. Here is a case, if not of concurrent endowment, at least of concurrent immunity, which comes to the same thing.

The fact is, that both Christian and heathen writers were interested in representing the change effected by the early Christian emperors as more complete than it was. To the Christian writer it was a point of honour to clear them from any stain of complicity with Paganism. To the heathen writer, wise after the event, the memory of those princes was naturally odious, and to exaggerate their hostility to the gods was to deepen the stain on their characters. But we have fortunately other witnesses quite free from suspicion. The coins, and the inscriptions, and the decrees, tell a very different tale. They show that in all essential respects Paganism, at least in the West, was as free to develop itself as before. They reveal to us temples built, priesthoods established, sacrifices offered, as hitherto; they exhibit the name of the Emperor connected with the worship of Jupiter the Preserver, of Mars the Champion, of Hercules the Conqueror, of Sol the Invincible. Hercules is still the preserver of Cæsar, and Sol is still the companion of Augustus. They show that the worship of the Lydian Cybele still flourished on the hill Vatican, and the worship of the Persian Mithras was still maintained in the vaults of the Capitol. All this it is necessary to bear in mind if we would understand the true position of Julian. It is quite a mistake to suppose that he had to begin *de novo*, and to re-establish Paganism. It still held the political vantage ground, however much it had lost in social prestige; and if it had had any inherent vitality at all, its work of restoration could have been as successful as in fact it proved futile.

What, then, was the real nature of the injury which this half-century of Christian supremacy in the person of the sovereign had inflicted on Paganism? First of all, the Imperial legislation, while it protected and even fostered the central institutions of Paganism, zealously assailed some outlying works. On two points especially it was uncompromising. It rigorously proscribed divination, and sternly repressed certain special rites accompanied by licentious orgies. In neither respect, however, did it go beyond what during the Republic and under the early emperors had again and again been held necessary to secure the safety of the city and the morals of the people. But however justifiable, according to heathen precedents, this legislation of the early Christian emperors had proved a fatal blow to heathendom, for it was just here that the ardour of popular religion had consecrated itself. The patient energy, the suggestive mysticism, even the immoral orgies of the Oriental religions, had been found to have an irresistible attraction, and the ancient rites of Greece and Rome, which seemed cold and passionless by their side, were deserted for these new favourites. They were, it was true, only the buttresses of the old polytheism. The original structure of Roman and Hellenic worship was untouched; but when the main building was crumbling with age the removal of these ancient supports which had shored it up was fatal, and it fell by its own weight.

But, secondly, the erection of a new capital was a not less deadly blow to Paganism. Rome was the central fortress of heathendom: to withdraw from it the Imperial Government was to deprive it of its ammunition. After the building of Constantinople, Rome still remained the formal official capital of the empire; but, practically, its influence was gone. It no longer guided deliberation; it simply recorded results. And not only was Paganism materially weakened by this transference, but at the same time Christianity was delivered from its fetters. Constantinople was a Christian city from the beginning. Paganism had here no prescriptive claim and no time-honoured prestige. So long as the Imperial Government remained at Rome, it found itself inextricably entangled in Paganism. Constantine had felt its merciless strength, and the foundation of a new capital was his escape from it.

Yet, after all, such weapons as these would have been quite ineffective, if Paganism had possessed any inherent vitality. The grip of death was already upon it before the arm of power was raised against it. It was as when, after long centuries, the tomb of some ancient king is laid open, the stately form, and the majestic features, and the royal robes are exposed to our view. For the moment he seems to be living still as he lived in history; but we look again, and we see only a handful of dust. Sealed in its sepulchre, the corpse might have preserved its outward form for ages still; but the air and the light were poured in upon it, and all at once it crumbles away. Paganism was confronted with Christianity, and it vanished.

The infancy of Julian had been dabbled in blood. His earliest recollections would carry him back to the time when fathers, brothers, uncles, cousins, all had fallen in one indiscriminate massacre. From this carnage he and his brother Gallus alone had escaped; he himself, so he believed, because he was too young to be feared, and his brother because he was then a sickly boy, and seemed not to have long to live. The odium of this foul crime, whether justly or unjustly, rested on his cousin, the Emperor Constantius. If Constantius had not directly ordered it, he was thought to have connived at it. Certainly he had been on the spot, and, whether for want of power or for want of will, he had not prevented it. The courtiers and attendants attempted to palliate his cousin's guilt to the child Julian. They represented to him that Constantius had been deceived; that he was unable to restrain the savage outbreak of the soldiers; that he suffered fearful pangs of remorse; that he attributed to this crime all the misfortunes of his after life. It seems plain from this account that the spectre of this ghastly massacre haunted Julian's childish memory. He could not but feel that the bare sword was hanging over his own neck.

Julian was left an orphan before he was seven years old. His mother had died a few months after his birth. His father had perished, as we have seen. For some years after the massacre, he appears to have resided at Constantinople. Of his brother Gallus we hear nothing during this period. Julian himself was placed under the charge of an old family servant—a Scythian, Mardonius by name, a strict and pedantic disciplinarian, but also a man of culture, as the sequel shows. Mardonius taught his pupil to keep his eyes fixed on the ground as he took his walks. He led him always to and fro to school by the same way, knowing no other himself, and preventing the lad from discovering any other. He strictly prohibited him from going to the theatre or the circus, and altogether filled his mind with a distaste for the popular amusements of his age. We hear nothing of companionship, nothing of outdoor exercise, nothing of the cheerfulness and the sympathy which are equally necessary with the moral discipline and the intellectual training for the proper expansion of child's faculties. Julian was not like other children. Whatever may have been his natural disposition, his education had never allowed him to be a boy. Human nature, more especially childish nature, must seek relief somewhere from hard conventional restraints. Where all the usual outlets are closed, the buoyancy and the enthusiasm of the child will devise some means of escape. The paradise of Julian's childish existence was made up of two things. First, his tutor Mardonius was an enthusiastic admirer of Homer. If he prevented him from playing in the field he took him to the leafy islands of Calypso, to the Cave of Circe and the Gardens of Alcinous. With a less intelligent child this might have bred a feeling of disgust; but Julian was quick, imaginative, absorbing, and here was field for his sensibility. And, again, though his walks might be confined to one city, and to one street in that city, yet no bounds could shut out the glories of the heavens above. We have Julian's own authority for saying that his childish imagination was profoundly impressed by their contemplation. "From my earliest days," he wrote long afterwards, "a strange yearning after the rays of the God, the Sun God, sunk into my soul; and thus from the time I was quite a little child, when I looked at the light of heaven, I was beside myself with ecstasy, so that not only would I look eagerly and fixedly on the sun, but at night also, when there was a cloudless and clear sky, I gave up everything at once, and was rivetted by the beauties of the heavens, no longer understanding anything that any one spoke to me, nor giving heed to myself what I was doing." These, then, were the two bright spots which relieved the gloom of his childish life—the literature of Greece and the contemplation of the heavens. How large an influence these early memories had on his later apostasy, it will not be difficult to imagine.

This went on for some years with slight interruptions, and then there was a complete change. It was apparently about the year 344, when Julian would be thirteen or fourteen years old, and Gallus eighteen or nineteen, that, by the Emperor's orders, the two brothers were carried away to Macellum, an imperial castle in the mountain districts of Cappadocia. There they spent the next six years of life in strict retirement. What may have been the reason of this change we are not told, but we can easily suspect. Gallus was now growing up to manhood. He was tall, well made, and handsome, with flowing auburn hair; not unlike his uncle, the great Constantine, as we may infer from the description of the two men. The suspicious temper of Constantius might take alarm lest this young man should become the centre of disaffection and treason. But, however this may be, the seclusion was complete. Julian speaks of it as banishment. To himself it was the worst kind of banishment. He was banished not only from the city and the court, about which probably he knew little and cared less, but he was banished also from his books and his teachers. The two brothers saw no one of their own rank; their domestics were their only associates. Gallus was no companion for Julian. He had no literary taste; notwithstanding his handsome looks he was coarse and violent, even ferociously brutal, in his disposition, as the sequel shows. The treatment of Julian during this critical period of his life must have been altogether injurious to the healthy development of his character. A cramped boyhood almost certainly produces a one-sided manhood.

At length, after six years of seclusion, the brothers were again set free. What was the motive of Constantine—whether he considered that they had been sufficiently restrained, or whether some conscientious scruples found their way into his heart—we cannot say. Gallus and Julian were summoned to Constantinople. Soon after this a formidable insurrection broke out in the West, and Constantius found it necessary to associate some one with him in the cares of the empire. Accordingly Gallus, then twenty-five years old, was nominated Cæsar, and appointed to the command of the East. The appointment was most disastrous. Now that he was free from control, the innate ferocity of his disposition revealed itself. He has been compared, and the comparison does him no injustice, to a bloodthirsty tiger, who has broken through the bars of his cage, and, enraged by long confinement, fiercely attacks every one who comes in his way. Complaints of his savage, turbulent administration came thick upon the ears of Constantius. There were also rumours of a disloyal conspiracy on the part of the new Cæsar. Constantius might, perhaps, have forgiven the misgovernment ; but the treason could not be overlooked. Gallus was recalled, stripped of the purple, and put to death without a hearing. Constantius had dyed his hand once more in the blood of Julian's kindred. Julian was left alone in the world, confronted by the tyrant. This happened in the year 354.

But while the caged passions of Gallus had

sought compensation in this savage outbreak, the caged intellect of Julian was running riot in its own way. For a time he seems to have enjoyed comparative freedom. At Constantinople, at Nicomedia, at Pergamos, at Ephesus, we hear of his attendance on philosophers, on rhetoricians, on teachers of all kinds. The jealousy of Constantius could look with complacency on his philosophical and literary ardour. An ungainly, enthusiastic, unpractical scholar was the last man whom he need fear as a rival. It was during this period of turbulent, energetic, unreflecting, intellectual activity that the change came upon him. Whatever might have been the religious feelings of his boyhood, it was only now that Paganism asserted its power over his mind. The incident that decided his apostasy is eminently characteristic of the man and of the period. It happened in the year 351, the same year as that in which Gallus was invested with the purple, when Julian himself was twenty years of age. In the course of conversation one of his teachers happened to speak of Maximus, a famous philosopher, whom he described as possessing great natural gifts, and as accompanying his teaching by demonstrations. Julian's curiosity was excited. He demanded an explanation. He was told that on one occasion Maximus, in the presence of the speaker and others, had burnt a grain of incense in the temple of Hecate and chanted some mysterious hymn, when suddenly they saw the statue of the goddess smile upon him. On their expressing surprise, he told them that they should see a greater marvel than this—the torches in the hands of the goddess should burst out into flames of their own accord. He had scarcely said the word when the lights burst out from the torches. "Stay with your books," said Julian, "and I wish you joy of them; I have found the man I have been seeking for." He sought out Maximus, and was initiated in his philosophy and his magic.

This grotesque and unnatural combination was, as I have said, characteristic of the man and of the age. In earlier times philosophy and popular superstition were deadly foes, but in face of Christianity both the one and the other had learnt their weakness, and this unequal alliance was patched up. The new Platonist philosophy adopted not only the mythology of Greece and Rome, but the nature-worship and the magic of the East. A true theology must appeal at once to the intellect which demands a reason for its allegiance, and to the religious instinct which is conscious of dependence on a higher power. Christianity recognises both these claims. Greek philosophy appealed to the one faculty; Pagan religion to the other. Thus divided they could do nothing, though the alliance was formed. It was well conceived, but it was impossible, because it was a fundamental violation of truth. Julian, the champion of heathendom, advanced to slay Christianity with philosophy in his right hand and superstition in his left, and both weapons shivered in his grasp.

Julian was a Pagan now, but he carefully concealed the change. During the next ten years, until the death of Constantius, this cloak of dissimulation was never thrown aside. The immediate outward effect of his conduct was a stricter attention to the services of the Church. The old fable, said his heathen friend Libanius afterwards, was here reversed, and the lion was clothed in the ass's skin. Only one or two most intimate friends were in the secret, but it was more widely suspected. Ardent Pagans began to look to him as the future restorer of Paganism; old prophecies were banded about that Christianity was soon to come to an end. One such oracle fixed the limit of 365 years for the worship of Christ. The term was fast drawing to a close. I shall not undertake the task of arraigning Julian as before the bar of the Eternal Righteousness. All such attempts to anticipate the verdict of the Great Judge must be as vain as they are presumptuous; but it is due to the nobler features of his character—and these were neither few nor insignificant—to dwell on the extenuating circumstances of his case. And surely no man's education was more faulty, or more likely to produce a disastrous revulsion.

Christianity was associated in his memory with everything that was gloomy, terrible, repulsive. Its champion, in his eyes, was his most deadly enemy, Constantius, who had shed the blood of his nearest kinsmen, and who was ready at any moment to shed his own blood when the occasion might demand. Writing of himself at a later date in apathetic allegory, he describes himself as a youth who, looking back upon the mass of evil that had befallen him from his own kinsmen and cousins, was so astounded that he resolved to throw himself down to Tartarus, but was rescued by Helios, the Sun God. This throws a flood of light on the personal influences which coloured his views of Christianity, and finally led to his apostasy. Moreover, the form of Christianity which was presented to him was not calculated to impress him deeply or favourably. The coldness of asceticism would take no firm hold of his ardent and enthusiastic nature. Its representatives, the Arian bishops, would not recommend the cause; the exceeding bitterness of theologic controversy called down his contempt, and the superstitious reverence for the bones of the martyrs aroused his disgust. In the allegory to which I have already alluded he speaks of himself as a child covered with filth and dirt, on whom the Sun God at length took pity. Whatever rays of light had burst the gloom of his earlier life were associated with the glories of nature.

While this strange revel of philosophy and fanaticism was going on in his mind, Julian visited Athens—Athens at once the home of Greek literature and the sanctuary of Pagan idolatry. No place more congenial to his temper could have been chosen than this. Here it was that he fell in with two devout Christian students, Gregory and Basil—names destined hereafter to be famous in the history of the Church. Gregory has left a description of the future emperor as he appeared at this time—a speaking likeness we cannot doubt. The convulsive movements of the shoulder, the half-scared, half-frenzied glance of the eye, the grotesque contortions of the face, the tumultuous, hesitating speech, the loud, immoderate laughter, the restlessness of the whole man from head to foot, seemed to Gregory to bode no good. Much of this was natural to Julian, but much, also, may have been due to the consciousness of the secret seething within his soul. We know what Gregory did not know—that Julian was a Pagan already when he was discussing Christian topics with Christian students.

But Julian's studies were rudely interrupted. Constantius again found the burden of the empire too heavy for his shoulders, and again he resolved to divide it. Julian, very reluctantly on his part, was appointed Cæsar, and charged with the administration of Gaul. He was now twenty-five years of age. The courtiers of Constantius laughed at the new Cæsar, and certainly the appointment did not give any fair promise of success. But this enthusiastic philosopher, this student recluse, soon showed that he had in him the making not only of an able ruler, but also of a consummate general. In vain the flatterers of Constantius ridiculed Julian's petty triumphs, as they were pleased to call them; in vain they dubbed him a scribbling Greek. Campaign after campaign added to his reputation. His administration of Gaul was unmistakably brilliant. So matters went on for five years, till the jealousy of Constantius brought about a crisis. An ill-judged attempt to withdraw Julian's best Gaulish troops produced a mutiny; the soldiers proclaimed him emperor, and he accepted the title. Having assumed the imperial purple, he marched to force his recognition on Constantius; but he was saved the peril of an appeal to arms. Fever anticipated the conflict, and carried off Constantius opportunely. Julian was now absolute emperor, master of himself and master of the world. He could throw off the mask at length; he was free to carry out his long cherished design for the restoration of Paganism. With what energy, with what devotion, with what fanaticism, with what futility he worked for this end it will be my business in my next and concluding lecture to describe.

III.*

THE history of Julian has been employed as an apologue by more than one writer when satirising some religious reaction of his day. A well-known living theological critic of Germany uses it as a cloak for an attack on the late King of Prussia, and English clergymen under the reign of James II., assailing the religious tendencies of the King, denounced him as another Julian the Apostate. Such comparisons may serve their immediate purpose, but they are almost always misleading, and may be very unjust. I think, however, that we may, with advantage, compare this Pagan reaction in the Roman empire under Julian with the Papal reaction in England under Mary. The two sovereigns, indeed, have little in common except their manifest sincerity, but the general relations and the ultimate effects of the two movements are not so very dissimilar. They both interposed after a very decided predominance of the opposite cause; they both were a return to the forms of the past; they both involved a reversal of the traditional policy of the reigning house; they both were short in duration, but resolute, uncompromising, energetic in action;

* Delivered in St. Paul's Cathedral, Tuesday evening, November 18th, 1873.

and they both proved utterly futile in the result, because they were unsupported by any deep feeling in the mass of the people. So far as they produced any effects at all, they served only to nerve the energies and reassure the confidence of their antagonists.

Julian was now thirty years old when the death of Constantius left him sole master of the Roman empire. In stature he was rather below the average height; his frame was muscular and strong; his shoulders were unusually broad; his neck was thick and arched; he had a bright and piercing eye—the family characteristic which was so remarkable in his uncle Constantine; the upper part of his face, the brow, and the nose were fine and well chiselled; his mouth was too large, and his lower lip hung disagreeably. He wore a rough, pointed beard, the usual appendage of philosophers. Of his personal appearance he was studiously careless. It would almost seem as though the courtly dignity and scrupulous neatness of his cousin Constantius had produced a revulsion in him. He ostentatiously vaunts his unpolished manner and his slovenly habits. He was signally undignified in all his gestures. Of his excitability and his restlessness of manner I have already spoken. He was a hurried, reckless talker. His tongue, we are told, was never at rest. His energy was enormous. During his administration of Gaul, when his days had been spent in the anxieties of government or in the toils of war, he would sit up half the night studying or writing. When he became Emperor his energy seemed only to increase. The great purpose of his life, the restoration and reform of Paganism, was now definitely before him, and he worked at it with a determination which never slackened. Into a short reign of eighteen months he crowded an amount of work which probably no sovereign has ever surpassed. He had on his shoulders the undivided weight of a great empire; he was preparing for a difficult and dangerous campaign; he was busied with the hopeless task of restoring an effete religion; he was writing hither and thither to the representatives of heathendom, scolding, stimulating, encouraging; and yet he found time for a vast amount of literary work besides. He corresponded with rhetoricians and philosophers; he composed orations and hymns in praise of heathen deities; he wrote a lengthy and elaborate attack on the Christian religion, and threw off light squibs on his contemporaries and on his predecessors. If his one fatal act of apostasy had not perverted and spoiled everything, he might have ranked among the greatest of princes. As it was, he has no claim to the title of greatness. He did nothing which has lived, because he did nothing which deserved to live. He left nothing, absolutely nothing, behind which has tended to make mankind happier, or better, or wiser.

Julian, if his own account may be believed, assumed the imperial diadem with the greatest reluctance; it was forced upon him by the soldiers before he knew where he was; and yet there is reason to believe that his coyness was in great measure affected. It is quite clear that he was already possessed of the idea of a Pagan restoration, and that he considered himself as having a special call from his gods for this work. The Genius of Rome, we are told, appeared to him in a vision. He reproached the reluctant Cæsar with having so often driven him from his doors, and threatened to depart for ever if he were excluded this time. Thus warned, Julian responded to the call; but he still continued to dissemble. We read of his praying to Mercury, of his receiving admonitions from Jupiter; we are told of his consulting auspices and using divination in private; and yet on the festival of the Epiphany, many months after he had been proclaimed Emperor, we find him entering a Christian Church, and there solemnly offering up his prayers to Almighty God. His heathen biographer and admirer assigns as the reason, that he might secure the allegiance of his Christian subjects. The strange thing is that neither Julian, nor Julian's friends, seemed to think any apology needed for this dissimulation. Much, indeed, should be forgiven to one who, from early childhood, had been driven by the cruelty of his lot to shield himself under an impenetrable reserve; but it is hard to understand the moral blindness which fails to see that this flagrant violation of truth had need to sue for forgiveness. Those martyrs whom Julian derided and despised held it a glorious gain to sacrifice life and all things rather than consent even to a momentary act which might be interpreted as a denial of their faith. I need not ask which is the loftier spectacle of the two.

But indeed Julian, notwithstanding the many noble features in his character—his justice, his moderation, his strict temperance, his unsparing energy—was wholly wanting in those higher graces which are the crown of the Christian character. He was egotistical in the extreme; his self-consciousnes rarely, if ever, deserts him; he will let all the world know that he is a model philosopher; he is always thanking his gods that he is not as other men are. Even when he satirises himself his irony is only a veil—a very thin veil, which rather suggests than conceals his self-complacency. He is always standing before the mirror, always soliciting the admiration of mankind. Of the childlike humility which is the main portal to the kingdom of heaven, he knows nothing. And yet with all this dissimulation and all this acting we should do the man a gross injustice if we imagined that he was insincere. Of his sincerity in the work which he undertook he gave every proof which it is possible for a man to give. He showed himself ready to spend and be spent for it. This strange combination of the enthusiast and the dissembler, of the fanatic and the philosopher, may be very difficult to realise; but there can be no doubt that they did unite in the person of Julian. In this spirit Julian applied himself to his task.

This task was two-fold. He must depress Christianity, and he must reanimate and reform Paganism. In his relation to Christianity he avowed himself on principle favourable to absolute toleration. "I do not wish the Galileans," he wrote, "to be put to death or to be beaten unjustly, or to suffer any other wrong. We ought rather to pity than to hate those who are unfortunate in matters of the greatest importance." How far this was the genuine dictate of his heart, and how far it was suggested by principles of expediency, we cannot tell, but at all events he could not persuade himself to apply his principle frankly. He restored a heretic bishop because his restoration would create divisions among Christians, and expelled the orthodox Athanasius because his presence was a tower of strength to the Church. The letters of Julian on this occasion betray the weakness of his position. He has absolutely nothing to allege against Athanasius except that he had taught men to treat the gods with contempt, and that he had dared to baptise Greek ladies of rank—in other words, that he was highly successful as a Christian missionary. Having no argument, he descends to abuse. He scolds the Alexandrians that petition him to rescind the decree of banishment: he reviles Athanasius himself; he calls him an impious villain, a vile Manichæan. He responds to their petition by expelling him not from Alexandria only, but from the whole of Egypt. Altogether there is a marked deterioration in Julian's character from the time when he becomes his own master. He had plainly supposed that he should carry everything before him: he had imagined that he had only to proclaim toleration, and his subjects would be as enamoured of Paganism as he himself was. He was grievously disappointed. He found in Christianity a strength, a vitality, a resistance for which he was not prepared. He found in Paganism a feebleness, an irresolution, an indifference, an utter absence of self-sacrifice, which contrasted strangely with his own devoted enthusiasm.

It is infinitely tragical to contemplate his gradually descending from the high level on which he took his stand at first to mean devices of all kinds—more tragical than though he had boldly taken up the sword of the persecutor at once. He would not desert his principle of toleration; he never ceased to enunciate that to the last; but he would connive at violations of it. Pagan outrages on the Christians were condoned or gently rebuked. When assaults on their life and their property were reported to him, he would say, flippantly, these Galileans—so he always called them—ought not to resent the opportunity of being made martyrs when they prized martyrdom so highly; that they had no just cause for complaint in being condemned to poverty when poverty was so loudly extolled in their Lord. But, indeed, Julian showed unmistakably by one enactment that toleration with him was not an inviolable principle. An edict was issued by him forbidding any Christian to give instruction in Greek literature under any circumstances. The reason assigned was that, as they did not believe in the gods of Homer and Hesiod, they were not fit expositors on these points. " Let them go," wrote the Emperor, "to the churches of the Galileans, and there expound Matthew and Luke." Among those condemned to silence by this decree were not a few of the most illustrious teachers of the age. It made a profound sensation at the time. It was most severely criticised by Julian's own heathen admirers at a later date. " It deserves," writes one, "to be buried in eternal silence." To what further lengths the intolerance of Julian might have gone as he realised more and more the bitterness of failure if his reign had been prolonged, we can only conjecture; but the descent was sufficiently rapid to suggest that, soured by disappointment, he might, had he lived, have been found at the last among the most relentless of persecutors.

But while he was thus employing every artifice to depress Christianity, he was also straining every nerve to reanimate and restore Paganism. "He was," says his heathen panegyrist, Libanius, "the best of priests as he was the first of Emperors." He valued the title of Chief Pontiff, we are told, more highly than the dignity of Emperor. As Chief Pontiff he made his influence felt throughout the empire, reopening temples, restoring privileges, reinstituting sacrifices. No deity and no rite in any corner of his dominions escaped his vigilance. Whether it was the worship of the Phrygian Cybele, or of the Apis at Memphis, or of the Daphnian Apollo at Antioch, his interest was equally unflagging. He was everywhere advising, coaxing, threatening, goading into activity, where he could not fan into enthusiasm. And not content with thus exercising his official superintendence, he was most assiduous in his own personal services. In season and out of season he would ply the bystander with questions as to his religious belief. In season and out of season he would dispute against the Galileans. Wherever he went the altars smoked with victims. He would offer sacrifices of a whole hecatomb at once. He ransacked land and sea for rare birds and beasts, that he might offer them in sacrifice to the gods. At Antioch his soldiers were constantly seen borne away from the temple through the streets, gorged and intoxicated, after the revelry of these religious festivals. All kinds of divination, by flight of birds, by the inspection of entrails, by the sound of waters, by oracular responses, and by Sibylline books, were diligently sought out.

Every charlatan who pretended to some new secret of soothsaying was welcomed by him. Strange to say, all this fervour of devotion did not recommend Julian to his heathen subjects. It shows the hollowness of Paganism at this time that his conduct was met either with ridicule or with condemnation. The common people called him in derision a victim butcher, and not a sacrificial priest. It was sneeringly said that if he had returned triumphant from his Persian expedition the whole race of cows must have become extinct. The devotion of the Emperor found no response in the mass of his subjects.

But Julian was not only a restorer, he was also a reformer of heathendom. Whether he was conscious of the difference or not, the Paganism which he had set up as his ideal was quite another thing from the Paganism which had been handed down from the past. He strove to graft the morality and the organisation of Christianity on the stem of heathendom. The priests of Paganism were merely the performers of certain rites, the depositories of certain mysteries. They had no moral, or educational, or philanthropic conscience. The Christian clergy, on the other hand, over and above their duties in the public services of the Church, were expected to be also the pastors and teachers, the guides and examples, the ministers of comfort, and the dispensers of alms to their flocks. Julian attempted to infuse this pastoral element into the Pagan priesthood, to which it was wholly foreign. In the letters which are extant the priests are enjoined by him to abstain from the theatre or the tavern; they are forbidden to engage in any degrading occupation; they are required to see that their wives, and children, and servants attend regularly on the service of the gods; they are told to imitate the grave demeanour and the benevolent hospitality of Christian bishops. "It is shameful," writes the Emperor, "that the impious Galileans should support our people as well as their own." Such a conception of the priest's office must have surprised Julian's correspondents. They had not bargained for anything of the kind.

But, with all his efforts, Julian made no real advance. There were, in large numbers, apostasies when he apostatised, just as there had been conversions when Constantine was converted; but these insincere adherents from fashion or self-interest are the weakness, not the strength, of any cause. Julian could not have deceived himself. He saw none of the self-sacrifice which is the only evidence of genuine religious conviction. He upbraided the crowds who flocked to the temples, not to worship the gods, but to applaud the Emperor.

And now the end was fast approaching. About Midsummer 362, Julian took up his residence at Antioch, where he spent nine months preparing for his Persian campaign. This sojourn aggravated his disappointment. The people of Antioch did not take kindly to their sovereign. Before long he had succeeded in making himself equally unpopular with both the great sections of the community. At Antioch, where Christianity had first obtained its name, the Christians formed an exceptionally large fraction of the whole population. They would not be predisposed favourably towards an apostate, and his injustice only served to confirm their hatred. A fire broke out in the temple of Apollo of Daphne, and it was burnt to the ground. Without any adequate reason his suspicions fell on the Christians; he put the suspected persons to cruel tortures, but elicited no confession. Thus foiled, he ordered the principal church of Antioch to be closed and razed to the ground. The attitude of the Christians was one of stern defiance. Under the walls of the palace, along the streets of the city, wherever the Emperor would be likely to hear, were chanted the words of the Psalmist—"Confounded be all they that worship carved images, and that delight in vain god. The idols of the heathen are silver and gold, even the work of men's hands. Eyes have they and see not. They that make them are like unto them, and so are all they that put their trust in them." Nor was he more fortunate with the heathen population. He and they were co-religionists, but his Paganism was not their Paganism. The theatrical exhibitions, the festive orgies, the dancing and the revelry, these were the very soul of religious worship to them. He despised all such things. They ridiculed the officious devotion with which he hurried from temple to temple and from altar to altar, present at every festival and participating in every rite. He took his revenge by satirising their ungodliness. He told them at the great festival of their patron god, the Daphnian Apollo, he had expected to see costly victims smoking on the altar, but found there only one miserable goose, the solitary offering of a poor priest. Indeed, he was doomed to disappointment on all sides. One great project which he entertained at this time was the rebuilding of the temple of Jerusalem. It was not that he loved the Jews, but that he hated the Christians. So he entered into communication with the Jewish patriarch, and the work was commenced. The ruined walls were demolished, the foundations of the new building begun; but as the workmen penetrated underground, great globes of fire burst out from the earth and drove them back. Again and again they renewed the attempt; again and again they were repulsed. The project was relinquished and the temple remains unbuilt to this day.

Thus irritated and disappointed, Julian left Antioch and commenced his march. At his departure he vented his anger against the offending people by declaring that he would not enter the city again, but on his return he would go to Tarsus instead. He was as good as his word. He did return to Tarsus; but he returned there a corpse. Disastrous omens, we are told, thronged upon him. During his march on Hierapolis, as he entered the city, a portico suddenly gave way, and crushed fifty soldiers under its ruins. At Davana a huge stack of straw fell, and smothered to death as many more. At Carrhæ, the fatal scene of the defeat of Crassus, he was troubled with sinister dreams. At Circesium he received letters from Sallust, the Prefect of Gaul, entreating him to suspend the ill-omened expedition. Here, too, was an apparition of sinister augury. The corpse of an executed criminal was found lying across the path. At another place an enormous lion confronted the soldiers across their path. He was shot by them, and presented to Julian. It portended the death of a king, but on the question what king was meant there was a division of opinion. The Etruscan soothsayers considered it a disastrous sign; the philosophers interpreted it favourably. The next day a soldier named Julianus was struck down by lightning. This omen again was differently explained. The soothsayers and the philosophers took opposite sides.

Arrived at the scene of conflict, the Emperor, after obtaining some successes, offered a magnificent sacrifice—ten fine bulls—to Mars the Avenger. The omens were unmistakably sinister. Julian was disgusted with the ingratitude of the god, and called Jupiter to witness that he would not sacrifice to Mars again; "nor," adds the historian, "did he belie his oath, being carried off prematurely by a speedy death." These prodigies, with others, are related by a Pagan who accompanied the army. Christian writers add an incident of which I see no reason to question the proof, and which certainly deserves to be true. Julian's common taunt against the Christians was their worship of a dead man. While preparing for his expedition at Antioch, he fell into dispute, after his manner, with a Christian whom he met accidentally, and said mockingly, "What is the Son of the carpenter doing now?" "He is making a coffin," was the prompt reply. The Son of the carpenter was making a coffin—a coffin not for Julian only, but for the Paganism of which Julian was the champion.

It is not necessary for me to follow out this

expedition to its disastrous issue. It is sufficient to say that Julian was inveigled, surrounded, pierced by a spear from some unknown Persian or Saracen hand. He perceived at once that he was mortally wounded. His words at this moment are differently reported. According to one account, he cried out, " Oh, Galilean, thou hast conquered ! " Another story relates that he took the blood welling from the wound in his hand, and flung it up towards the sun, his patron god, with an imprecation—" There, take thy fill." Neither saying, perhaps, is reported on sufficiently good authority, but either would accord well with the disappointment and irritation which marked the closing scenes of his life. He inquired what was the name of the place. It was a small village called Parthia. He had been forewarned long ago that in Parthia he should die. He had supposed that the famous country of that name was meant. We are reminded by this incident of an English sovereign lying on his death-bed in the famous chamber at Westminster, which still bears the name of Jerusalem. " It hath been prophesied to me many years I should not die but at Jerusalem, which vainly I supposed the Holy Land." Within a few hours Julian had breathed his last. He died on the 26th June, 363, being not yet quite thirty-two years old, and with him perished the last and best hope of Paganism. Less than twenty years after, the Emperor Gratian refused the title of Supreme Pontiff. This was the first overt act of disestablishment. Then blow followed blow in rapid succession. Paganism was first disestablished, then disendowed, then prohibited; yet it still continued to linger on till at length it was buried in the grave of the empire. St. Augustine's *City of God* was the pæan of victory over the enemy slain. Julian's work had been found like a child's castle elaborately piled up of sand on the brink of the ocean. The rising tide advanced steadily, inexorably, relentlessly, and no traces of the structure remain.

WOMAN AND THE GOSPEL.*

"And He took the damsel by the hand."—MARK v. 41.

IN selecting this text I have no intention of saying many words on the actual scene itself. The raising of Jairus's daughter attracts our attention by its vivid narrative, and by its intense human pathos, while the two foreign words, summing up the interest of the story, linger strangely in our ears, impressing it effectually on our memories. Nor, again, do I purpose speaking of its direct theological

* Preached in St. Paul's Cathedral, Thursday, June 19th, 1884, on the anniversary of the Girls' Friendly Society.

import, whether as an answer to human faith, or as a manifestation of the Divine power. In this latter aspect this is one of three signal miracles, the anticipations of Christ's own resurrection. It claims, and it has received, the most earnest study, both in itself and in relation to other incidents of the same class.

These more obvious aspects of the text are beside my present purpose. I wish to-day to treat it from a wholly different point of view. Christ's miracles have always the highest spiritual significance. They are not miracles only, but parables also. The Messiah's kingdom would have achieved comparatively little for mankind if it had brought deliverance to the captive in a literal sense only. A far heavier and more galling bondage would still remain—the bondage of sin. Physical blindness is only a type of moral blindness; Christ's healing power in the one case is the pledge of His healing power in the other. The palsy of the body symbolises the palsy of the soul. If the paralytic is bidden to take up his bed and walk, this is before all things an assurance to us that Christ is able and willing to heal the paralysis of the soul. From this point of view the words of the text are full of meaning to all who are met together to-day. "He took the damsel by the hand, and said unto her, Damsel, I say unto thee, Arise. And straightway the damsel arose, and walked; and they were astonished with a great astonishment."

Need I remind you that this is the earliest miracle of raising the dead recounted in the Gospels? Two others follow. The widow of Nain and the sisters of Bethany receive back their dead. But the one was a growing youth, the other was a man of mature age. The young woman was Christ's first miracle of resurrection. On her was wrought first this stupendous miracle. For her was won this earliest triumph over death and hell. Is not this a significant fact in itself, but especially significant for you, for it proclaims the fundamental principle of the Gospel charter? It announces that the weak and the helpless in years, in sex, in social status, are especially Christ's care. It declares emphatically that in Him is neither male nor female. It is a call to you, you women-workers, to do a sister's part to these your sisters. Christ's action in this miracle is a foreshadowing of His action in the Church. The Master found woman deposed from her proper social position. The man had suffered not less than the woman by this her humiliation. Jew and Gentile had conspired together in an unconscious conspiracy to bring about this disastrous result. The Hebrew Rabbi and the Greek philosopher alike had gone astray. It is the recorded saying of a famous Jewish doctor that the words of the law were better burned than committed to woman. It is an opinion ascribed to the most famous Athenian statesman, that woman had then achieved her highest glory when her name was heard amongst men least, either for virtue or for reproach. A moral resurrection was needed for womanhood. It might seem to the looker-on like a social death, from which there was no awakening, but it was only the suspension of her proper faculties and opportunities, a long sleep from which a revival must come sooner or later. It was for Him, and Him alone, who was the Vanquisher of death, who has the keys of Hades— for Him alone to open the door of her sepulchral prison and resuscitate her dormant life and restore her to her ordinary place in society. When all hope was gone, He took her by the hand and bid her arise; and at the sound of His voice and the touch of His hand she arose and walked, and the world was astonished with a great astonishment. We ourselves are so familiar with the results, the position of woman is so fully recognised by us, it is bearing so abundant fruit every day and everywhere, that we overlook the magnitude of the change itself. Only, then, when we turn to the harem and the zenana do we learn to estimate what the Gospel has achieved, and has still to achieve, in the emancipation of woman, and her restitution to her lawful place in the social order. To ourselves the large place which woman occupies in the Gospel and in the early apostolic history seems only natural. To contemporaries it must have appeared in the light of a social revolution. The very opening of the Gospel is charged with

Divine messages communicated to us through woman—Mary, Elizabeth, Anna; women attend our Lord everywhere during His earthly ministry. The sisters, Martha and Mary, are set before us as embodying the two contrasted types of character, the practical and the contemplative. To a woman, and to a woman alone, is given the promise of an undying hope beyond the glory of the mightiest earthly princes. Of her it is said: "Wheresoever this Gospel is preached in the whole world, there shall this which this woman has done be told as a memorial of her." To a woman were spoken those gracious words of pardon most tender and compassionate, the consolation and the stay and the hope of the penitent to all time: "Her sins, which are many, are forgiven, for she loveth much." Women are the chief attendants at the crucifixion, and the chief ministrants at the tomb. Woman is the first witness of the resurrection; and as it was in Christ's personal ministry, so it is in all the Apostolic Church. In the first gathering of the little band after the Ascension, women are found assembled with the apostles. This is a foreshadowing of the part which they are destined to play in the subsequent narrative of the history of the Church. Cast your eyes down the salutations in the Epistle to the Romans. There is Phœbe, a deaconess of the Church of Cenchrea, commended as having been the succourer of many, among others of the Apostle himself. There is Priscilla, who with her husband had laid down her neck for his life, to whom he himself not only gave thanks, but all the Churches of the Gentiles. There is Mary, who bestowed much labour upon him and others; Tryphena and Tryphosa, who laboured much in the Lord. There is Persis, to whom the same testimony is borne. There is the mother of Rufus, who had also been like a mother to himself. There is Julia, and there is the sister of Nereus. A long catalogue to appear in the salutations of a single epistle!

Turn again from the Church of which St. Paul knew least when he wrote, to the Church of which he knew most. Witness his relation to his beloved Philippian Church. He addresses himself first to the women who resort to the places of prayer among the individual women with whom he came in contact. At Philippi we read of Lydia, his earliest hostess in this city, of the damsel from whom he cast out a spirit of divination, and then of Euodias and Syntyche, women who laboured with him in the Gospel; and indeed we know more of the women at Philippi than we know of the men.

But it was not only this desultory, unrecognised service, however frequent, however great, that women rendered to the spread of the Gospel in its earliest days. The Apostolic Church had its organised ministrations of women, its order of deaconesses, its order of widows. Women had their definite place in the ecclesiastical system of those early times, and in our own age and country again the awakened activity of the Church is once more demanding the recognition of the female ministry. The Church feels herself maimed of one of her hands. No longer she fails to employ, to organise, to consecrate to the service of Christ, the love, the sympathy, the tact, the self-devotion of women. Hence the revival of the female diaconate in its multiplication of sisterhoods. But these, though the most definite, are not the most extensive developments of this revival. Everywhere institutions are springing up, manifold in form and purpose, for the organisation of women's work. There has been, and there is still, a shameful waste of this latent power, boundless in its capacities if only fostered and developed. The famous heroines of womanhood will necessarily be few. It is rarely women's part to save a city or guide a church. Only at long intervals on the stage of the history of the world appear such women as Joan of Arc; but here and there God raises up an exceptional heroine to do exceptional work, which a woman alone can do, or do so effectually, for her age and country. But generally it is in the quieter, less obtrusive, more homely, and more womanly way, that she is called to test her power, certainly not less real or less beneficent, though it may be less striking, than the power of man. She is a mother in her own household, her own kindred, her own parish, her own neighbourhood; the guide, the helper of man. Yes; a priestess and a prophetess to the young, the sick, the frail and erring, the poor and needy—needy whether of spiritual or bodily healing. It is the province of the Church, when acting by the Spirit and in the name of Christ, to develop the power of women, to take by the hand and raise from its torpor that which seemed a death, but which is only a sleep; and now, as then, revived life and beneficent work will amaze the looker-on—"they were astonished with a great astonishment."

Among the most recent developments of the work of the Church of Christ your Girls' Friendly Society has taken a foremost place. I would say in all sincerity, that when I read your last report with profound joy and thankfulness, I was impressed, no less by the completeness of your ideal, than by the variety and expansion of your work. I do not say this to commend; this is not the time or the place for commendation. "Not unto us, O Lord, not unto us, but unto Thy name give the praise." You will not be content, will you? you will not be content, if you are true to your ideals, with holding out the hand of loving sympathy in your own home and neighbourhood to a humble sister needing a sister's care and guidance? Your love will follow her about that she may never be lost sight of. It is a trite complaint that in this day the old relations between master and servant have vanished, or almost vanished away. The bond is no longer one of reciprocal loyalty, but of common convenience. Hence it is liable to severance at any moment in the feverish, ever-restless, fluctuating conditions of modern life. It was impossible that these relations should remain unchanged while all else was changing. The domestic servant or the shop girl has no longer a fixed home; she is a wanderer on the earth. It is just here that the catholicity of your plan should step in and counteract the evil. It is your part to realise this catholicity. When a girl once enrolls herself in your numbers, she is *yours*; everywhere, whithersoever she may go, the friendly eye will rest upon her; the friendly hand will be stretched out to her wheresoever she may be. She will find everywhere a home, because she will find everywhere friends. You cannot set this ideal before yourselves too definitely, or strive to realise it too earnestly.

Do you ask how your work may be truly effective? I answer you in the words of the text, "He took the damsel by the hand." There must be an intensity of human sympathy, and there must be an indwelling of the Divine power. The lesson of the miracle which I have taken for my starting-point involves both these ideals. The current of womanly sympathy must flow out deep and strong and clear. Is not this the typical meaning of Christ's action in the text? The touch of His warm hand restores the circulation and revives the life in those pale, motionless, death-like limbs. We want sympathy here, sympathy first and sympathy last—sympathy reflecting, however faintly, Christ's own boundless compassion and love. The cold, mechanical formalism of the relieving officer will not suffice; the haughty assertion of superiority, the condescending patronage of the fine lady will be worse than nothing. You must be a sister to your sisters, treading in the footsteps of your Brother, Jesus Christ. Is not this also the meaning of those words which He utters to the girl lying helpless before Him? He speaks to her not in the Greek, the conventional language of outward life, but in the Syriac, the true language of the family and the home. It pierces her, notwithstanding her death-like slumber. He speaks to her, as He speaks to us all, with the voice of a direct personal love. This is always the language of Christ's words, the language of Christ's Gospel,—" How hear we every man in our own tongue wherein we were born?"

And over and above all this, animating, inspiring, sanctifying your human sympathies, there must be the consciousness of the Divine presence, the sense of the Divine energy, in your work. You will apply yourself to it with a strength not your own; the power of the living Christ will thrill through you. Is not this the interpretation of the symbolic action, "He took the damsel by the hand"?—He *Himself*, and not another. "Not I, but Christ in me," will be the inspiring motive of your work, as it was in St. Paul's. *His* hand must guide your hand; nay, His hand must replace your hand, if the touch shall raise the damsel, and restore her to a better and a happier life.

And restore her it will; this intense human sympathy inspired by this consciousness of the Divine indwelling. It never has failed yet, and it never can fail to work miracles of resurrection and healing, in her helplessness, in her temptations, in all her struggles and perplexities, her bodily wants, and her spiritual trials. It will be to her comfort and strength and hope; it will throb her with the pulse of an awakened life.

But I have spoken hitherto as if these helpless girls whom you befriend were the sole counterparts of Jairus's daughter. I have regarded them as only the patients whom Christ's awakening hands raise from their death-like slumbers. Is this an adequate representation of the case, think you? Are there not others even more needy than they of this beneficent movement? Are we not taught on the highest authority that it is more blessed to give than to receive? But, if so, have we not a truer antitype of this damsel whom Christ raised in these befriended girls? Yes, Christ has taken them by the hand, and has revived them, has awakened them from the heavy, death-like slumber of a selfish, self-contained being. Christ has shown them the beauty and the power of sympathy, and it has been to them the throbbing of a new life. Surely it is not only the daughters of ancestral lineage and of Norman blood, not only a Clara Vere de Vere, who are sickening with a disease, and who need Christ's healing hand; is there not in the home of the professional man many a daughter and many a sister on whose hand time hangs heavily, whose life is wasting away, fretting with feverish excitement, or sunk in self-indulgence and apathy, weary of self, and weary of others? How shall they wake up from their barren monotony and death-like existence? Sympathy, active sympathy for others; this, and this alone, can restore them. Mothers, train your daughters early to think for others, to care for others, to minister to others. Be assured this will be the most valuable part of their education. This heaven-born charity is the sovereign antidote to all the ills of womanhood. Is it some secret sorrow gnawing at the heart, some outraged feeling, or some harrowing bereavement, or some actual disappointment? Merge and absorb it in active solicitude for others. Is it some fierce temptation which shamed you, and each fresh struggle seems to leave you weaker than before? There will be no room for this if you devote yourself to the needs of others. All sin is selfishness in some form or other. Forget sloth; this is the best safeguard against temptation.

I appeal confidently to all those who have made the trial to say whether this medicine has healed them where all other medicines have failed? And, why, why? It is Christ's own love constraining them; it is Christ's own touch thrilling through their veins; hence they mark the resurrection—" He took the damsel by the hand; and straightway she arose and walked.'

PILATE.*

"Pilate saith unto Him, What is truth?"—JOHN xviii. 38.

ST. JOHN is especially distinguished among the four evangelists for his subtle delineation of character. We do not commonly remember—it costs us an effort to remember—how very largely we are indebted to the fourth gospel for our conceptions of the chief personages who bear a part in evangelical history, where those conceptions are most clear and distinct. If we analyse the sources of our information, we find again and again that while something is told us about particular persons in the other evangelists, yet it is St. John who gives those touches to the picture which make it stand out with its own individuality as a real, living, speaking man. The other evangelist will record a name, or, perhaps, an incident; St. John

* Preached in St. Paul's Cathedral, on Sunday Afternoon, May 30th, 1875, before some of Her Majesty's Judges, the Lord Mayor, and members of the Corporation of the City of London.

will add one or two sayings; and the whole person is instinct with life. The character flashes out in half-a-dozen words. "From the abundance of the heart the mouth speaketh." So it is with Philip, with Thomas, with Mary and Martha, and with several others who might be named. This vividness of portraiture is our strongest assurance, if assurance were needed, that the narrative was indeed written by him whose name it bears—by the beloved disciple and eye-witness himself. For, observe, there is no effort at delineation of character; there is no delineation of character at all, properly so called. The evangelist does not describe the persons whom he introduces; they describe themselves. The incidental act, the incidental movement or gesture, the incidental saying, tells the tale. That which he had heard, that which he had looked upon and his eyes had seen, that which his hands had handled of the Word of Life—that and that only he declared.

Pilate furnishes a remarkable illustration of this feature in St. John's gospel. Pilate is the chief agent in the crowning scene of evangelical history. He is necessarily a prominent figure in all the four narratives of this crisis. In the first three gospels we learn much about him. We find him there, as we find him in St. John, at cross purposes with the Jews. He is represented there, not less than by St. John, as giving an unwilling consent to the judicial murder of Jesus. His Roman sense of justice is too strong to allow him to yield without an effort. His personal courage is too weak to persevere in the struggle when the consequences threaten to become inconvenient. He is timid, politic, time-serving, as represented by all alike. He has just enough conscience to wish to shake off the responsibility, but far too little conscience to shrink from committing the sin. But in St. John's narrative we pierce far below the surface. Here he is revealed to us as the sarcastic, cynical worldling, who doubts everything, distrusts everything, despises everything. He has an intense scorn for the Jews, and yet he has a craven dread of them. He has a certain professional regard for justice, and yet he has no real belief in truth or honour. Throughout he manifests a malicious irony in his conduct at this crisis. There is a lofty scorn in his answer when he repudiates any sympathy with the accusers. "Am I a Jew?" There is a sarcastic pity in the question which he addresses to the Prisoner before him, "Art Thou the King of the Jews? Art Thou, then, a king—Thou poor, weak, helpless fanatic, whom with a single word I could doom to death?" He is half-bewildered with the incongruity of the claim; and yet there is a certain propriety that a wild enthusiast should assert his sovereignty over a nation of bigots; so he sarcastically adopts the title. "Will you that I release unto you the King of the Jews?" Even when, at length, he is obliged to yield to the popular clamour, he will at least have his revenge by a studied contempt. "Behold your King! Shall I crucify your King?" And to the very last moment he indulges his cynical scorn. The title on the cross was, indeed, unconsciously, a proclamation of a Divine truth; but in its immediate purpose and intent it was the mere gratification of Pilate's sarcastic humour. "Jesus of Nazareth." Could any good thing come out of Nazareth? "Jesus of Nazareth, the King of the Jews." He has sacrificed his honour to them, but he will not sacrifice his contempt. "What I have written, I have written."

But it is more especially in the sentence which I have chosen for my text that the whole character of the man is revealed. The Prisoner before him had accepted the title of a King. He based His claim to this title on the fact that He had come to bear witness of the truth. He declared that those who were themselves of the truth would acknowledge His claim. They were His rightful subjects; they were the enfranchised citizens of His kingdom.

Strange language this, in the ears of a cynical, worldly sceptic, to whom the most attractive hope of humanity was a judicious admixture of force and fraud. " Pilate saith unto Him, What is truth? And when he had said this he went out." The altercation could be carried no farther. Was not human life itself one great query without an answer? What was truth? "Truth"? This helpless Prisoner claimed to be a King, and He appealed, forsooth, to His truthfulness as the credential of His sovereign rights! Was ever any claim more contradictory of all human experience, more palpably absurd, than this? "Truth"? When had truth anything to do with founding a kingdom? The mighty engine of imperial power, the armed sceptre which ruled the world, whence came it? Certainly it owed nothing to truth. Had not Augustus established his sovereignty by an unscrupulous use of force, and maintained it by an astute use of artifice? And his successor, the present occupant of the imperial throne, was he not an arch dissembler, the darkest of all dark enigmas? The name of Tiberius was a byword for impenetrable disguise. Truth might do well enough for fools and enthusiasts; but for rulers, for diplomatists, for men of the world, it was the wildest of all wild dreams. "Truth"? What was truth? He had lived too long in the world to trust to any such hollow delusion. He had listened to the ceaseless din of philosophical disputations till he was weary of them. The Stoics, the Epicureans, the Platonists, all had their several specifics which they vended as truth. All were equally sure, and yet no two agreed.

He had witnessed, certainly not without contempt, and yet not altogether without dismay, the rising flood of foreign superstition—Greek, Syrian, Egyptian, Chaldean—which threatened to deluge the city and empire, and destroy all the ancient landmarks. Could he believe all or any of these? In this never-ending conflict of philosophical dogmas and religious creeds, what could he do but resign himself to scepticism, to indifference, to a cold and cynical scorn of all enthusiastic convictions and all definite beliefs? "What is truth?"

And yet as he turned away, neither expecting nor desiring an answer to a question which he had asked merely to end an inconvenient controversy, some uneasy misgivings, we may well suppose, flashed across the mind of this proud, sarcastic worldling, that he was now brought face to face with truth as he had never been brought before. There was a reality about every word and action of this Jewish Prisoner which arrested and overawed him. The calmness with which He urged His claims, the fearlessness with which He defied death, the impressive words, the still more impressive silence, the manifest innocence and rectitude of the Man, if he saw nothing more—these could not be without their effect even on a Pilate, steeped as he was in the moral recklessness and the religious despair of his age. At all events, he would serve the Man if he conveniently could.

But there had been also a nobler element in Pilate's education than moral scepticism and religious unbelief. He was a Roman governor, and as a Roman governor he was an administrator of Roman law. It was their appreciation of law, their respect for law, their study of law, far more than anything else, which gave its greatness to the character of the Roman people. Even in the most degraded ages of their history, and with the worst individual types of men, this is the one bright spot which relieves the gloom. It is the nobler prerogative of law to set a standard clear, definite, and precise. I have no concern here with other obligations to the law which as Christians we are bound to acknowledge, though, speaking before the chief representatives of English law and justice, I cannot fail to be reminded of them this afternoon. But this exhibition of a moral standard is a gain which it is hardly possible to over-estimate. The standard will not always be the highest. From the nature of the case it cannot be so. Law deals with some departments of morality very imperfectly; with others it does not attempt to deal at all. But still, whenever it is felt, and so far as it penetrates, it creates an ideal, and begets a habit which will not be powerless even with the most indifferent and reckless of men. So it was with Pilate. Theological scepticism had eaten out his religious principles to the very core. Unscrupulous worldliness and self-seeking had shattered his moral constitution; but though his principles were gone, and his character was ruined, still he was haunted by some lingering sense of professional honour; still the magnificent ideal of Roman justice and Roman law rose up before him, and would not lightly be thrust aside. He pleads repeatedly for justice against the relentless accusers. Three times he declares the Prisoner's innocence in the same explicit words—"I find no fault in Him." Once and again he strives to shift the responsibility from his own shoulders to theirs. "Take ye Him and judge Him according to your law. Take ye Him and crucify Him." But his efforts are all in vain. They will have none of this. The deed shall be done, and he shall do it.

It was not the first, and it would not be the last time that Pilate found himself in conflict with the Jews. For ten years he was governor of this turbulent, intractable people. This was an unusually long period of office under an Emperor like Tiberius, who was constantly changing his provincial governors from mere suspicion and distrust. It must have cost Pilate no little trouble to steer his course so long and so successfully, without foundering either on the suspicions of his jealous master here or on the bigotry of his stubborn subjects there. And yet he was constantly wounding the religious susceptibilities of the Jews. At one time he shocked them by bringing the military ensigns with the effigies of Cæsar within the walls of Jerusalem; at another he persisted in setting up some gilt shields, inscribed with a profane heathen dedication, in the palace of Herod within the holy precincts. In both cases he drove the Jews to the extreme verge of exasperation. In both cases he exhibits the same sarcastic and defiant scorn which is apparent here. In both cases their obstinate zeal or bigotry triumphs, as it triumphs here, and he is forced, in the end, to retrace his steps and to undo his deed.

So, then, this was only one brief episode in a protracted struggle between Pilate and the Jewish people. Doubtless, it seemed at the time quite insignificant compared with those other and fiercer conflicts in which he was engaged. It is passed over in silence by contemporary Jewish writers. It concerned the life of a single person only; it was settled in a single night; and yet it involved nothing less than the eternal destiny of all mankind.

Ah, there is a terrible irony in God's retributive justice, which so blinds a man to the true proportions of things. A single moment may do a wrong which centuries cannot repair. It is a dangerous thing to defy the truth. The majesty of truth is inviolable, and he who insults it in a moment of recklessness can never forecast the consequences. Time and space and notoriety are no measure of importance here. The most important criminal trial on record in the history of mankind was hurried through in two or three short hours, under cover of night and in the grey of early dawn.

This is the great lesson of Pilate's crime. He was surprised by the truth; he found himself unexpectedly confronted by the truth; and he could not recognise it. His whole life long he had tampered with truth; he had despised truth; he had despaired of truth. Truth was the last thing which he had set before him as the main aim of life. He had thought much of policy, of artifice, of fraud, of force; but for truth in any of its manifold forms he had cared just nothing at all. And his sin had worked out its own retribution. Not truth only, but the very Truth itself, Truth incarnate, stood before him in a human form, and he was blind to it; he scorned it; he played with it; he thrust it aside; he condemned, and he gibbeted it. "Suffered under Pontius Pilate," is the legend of eternal infamy with which history has branded his name.

So it is always. The Lord appears suddenly in His temple—in the shrine of the human heart and conscience; suddenly—at a time and in a form which we least expect. The truth visits us very frequently under the disguise of some common event, or some insignificant person. It surprises us, perhaps, in the accidental saying of some little child, or in the insidiousness of some mean temptation, or in the emergency of some trivial choice. It stands before us at once as our suppliant and our king. We fail to see its majesty veiled in its humble garb. We treat it as our prisoner when, in fact, it is our judge, and may become our gaoler. We flatter ourselves that we have power to condemn or to release it. We have no fault to find with it, but still we reject it; we crucify it; and before three days are gone it rises from its grave to bear eternal testimony against us. We could not see the truth, because we ourselves were not of the truth. Here in this judicial blindness is the warning of Pilate's example. Like is drawn to like : like only understands like. The truth is only for the children of truth.

We must not, however, unduly narrow the sense of truth and of truthfulness. When our Lord called Himself the truth—when He declared that the truth should make us free, He meant very much more than is commonly understood by the word. Veracity is, indeed, truth ; but it is only a small part of the truth. A man may be scrupulously veracious, strictly a man of honour ; he may always say what he believes ; he may always perform what he promises ; and yet he may not be, in the highest sense, true. He may be the slave of a thousand unrealities. A genuine child of truth is very much more than a speaker of the truth. He is a doer of the truth, and a thinker of the truth, and a liver of the truth. He is frank, open, and real in all things. Reality is the very soul of his being. He cares for nothing which is hollow, shadowy, superficial. Popularity, wealth, success, worldly ambition, and display are essentially unreal, because they are external, because they are transient. Therefore, he estimates them at their true value. The devotion of scientific men in pursuit of scientific truth wins our highest admiration. It is not without a thrill of national pride that we have just bidden God-speed to the gallant company which has started for the Arctic seas. To face untold hardships and possible death in such a cause is a worthy and noble aim, for these are realities. But obviously there are truths of far higher moment to the temporal and eternal well-being of man than the laws of electricity, or the causes of the Aurora, or the fauna of the Polar seas. Whence came I? Whither go I? What is sin? What is conscience? Is there a God in heaven? Is there a providence, a moral government, a judgment? Is there a redemption, a sanctification, a life eternal? These are the momentous, the pressing questions which a man can only shelve at his peril. Christ is the answer to all these questions. Therefore, He is the verity of verities. Therefore, He claims for Himself the title of the truth as His absolute and indefeasible right.

An incapacity to see the truth, when thus presented to us in its highest form, may arise from different causes. It may spring from bigoted partisanship, and religious pride, and obstinate formalism, as in the case of the Jews; or it may spring from cold cynicism, and worldliness, and dishonesty, as in the case of Pilate. These two conspire to crucify the truth. As we sow, so also shall we reap. Pilate's life had been stained in untruthfulness. His government had been an alternation of violence and artifice. His aim had not been to rule uprightly, to rule generously, but to rule at any cost. He must calm the suspicions of his jealous master, and he must quell the turbulence of an unruly people. Whatever means would conduce to these ends were to him legitimate means. Uprightness, honour, frankness, generosity, truth—what were these to him? He had no belief in them, and why should he practise them? He projected his own motives into his estimate of mankind at large. He read the characters of others in the distorted mirror of his own consciousness. Human life, as he viewed it, was false from beginning to end. It was, after all, the reflection of his own falsehood which he saw. He was ever looking out for the unrealities of existence. He had no eye for its realities. Men's convictions were their foibles: men's beliefs were his playthings. Untruthfulness, cynicism, distrust, scorn, had withered his soul. They only will find the truth who believe that the truth may be found. Pilate had no such belief. He had gone through life asking, half in bitterness, half in jest, "What is truth?" He had asked it now again, and the question was fatal. Pilate's temper of mind is a very real danger in an age like ours. Let us beware of thus jesting with truth, lest some time, like him, we crucify the truth unawares.

THE PHARISEE AND THE PUBLICAN.*

"Two men went up into the temple to pray."—LUKE xviii. 10.

THE teaching of the gospels is, in large portions, a teaching by contrast. This is the case, to a certain extent, in the historical narrative, but it is especially so in the parables of our Lord. Thus we have the contrast of the two brothers in the parable of the Prodigal Son; the contrast of the two sons in the parable of the father's vineyard; the contrast of the rich man and the beggar in the parable of Lazarus and Dives, and the like; the right and the wrong way of acting are figured, are embodied, are personified in two living, acting men. So it is here; the right and the wrong spirit in prayer, the right and the wrong attitude towards God, are set before us in portraits of imaginary men who might very well have been real men. If you had gone up to the temple any day, and watched the worshippers there, you might very likely have seen the counterpart both of the one and of the other. But there is not

* Preached in St. Paul's Cathedral, February 1st, 1884.

only a contrast in the parable, there is also a paradox, a surprise; the ordinary estimate of worth is set aside; the judgment of God overrules the judgment of men; the praise is given where men would give the blame, and the blame is given where men would give the praise. The object of the parable is to correct, to cancel, to reverse human judgment.

"Two men went up into the temple to pray." The place is the same, the time is the same, the object is the same; only the characters of the two men are widely different. To which will you give the preference? Could any pious Jew have doubted about his answer to this question? Would you yourself have doubted if you had been a Jew and lived in that age? Let us look more narrowly at these two men as they stand praying within the sacred precincts. Here is the one, a Pharisee. The sect to which he belongs is eminently religious, eminently patriotic; the law of God is their study day and night; their daily life is regulated on the strictest principles; they are the recognised leaders of their countrymen, their religious teachers and their political guides; they are regarded as the great bulwark against foreign tyranny and heathen idolatry; they have altogether the confidence of the people. And he is an eminently favourable type of the sect. It is not enough that he avoids gross and flagrant crime; that he is upright in his dealings with his fellow-men; that he respects the sanctity of the marriage vows;—he goes very far beyond this: he fasts regularly, he pays tithes scrupulously, he prays fervently after a manner, as this incident shows; not a suspicion is breathed against the truth of his statements as he thus describes himself. No doubt they were strictly true; the very point of the parable depends upon their accuracy. What more, then, would you have than this? Now, turn to the other worshipper, the publican. What a contrast we have here! The publicans were hated, despised, loathed by the Jews. There was only too much reason for all this hatred and contempt. The publicans were so called because they farmed the public taxes. The Roman masters let out the collection of the taxes for so much to the publicans, and the publicans made what they could by the collecting. Hence their position was unsatisfactory from first to last. Though Jews themselves, they were the representatives of the Roman masters of Judea. They thus reminded their fellow-countrymen at every turn of the galling yoke of a foreign tyranny, of a heathen tyranny, too. This made matters worse. Religion as well as patriotism was grievously compromised by them. This was bad enough; but this was not all. From the manner in which they contracted with the Roman government they were tempted to extortion and fraud. Their profits depended on petty acts of insolence and overreaching, and there is every reason to believe that, as a class, they did yield to their temptation. It might be said that their hand was against every man and evey man's hand was against them. Remembering these facts, we are able the more truly to honour a Matthew or a Zaccheus, towering far above the moral standard of their class. And the man before us—what shall we say of him? He had yielded to these temptations. Just as in the case of the Pharisee, so in the case of the publican, there is every reason to accept as strictly true his description of himself.

As I have said before, the very force of the parable depends on the truth of this statement. He, doubtless, had been extortionate; he had used his position and his power to oppress and defraud his fellow-countrymen. He was, perhaps, conscious, besides, of other grievous sins—not specially sins of his class, but sins of himself, sins of mankind. There can be little doubt that when he beat upon his breast, when he bewailed his sinfulness, when he entreated God's mercy, he had on his conscience some heavier weight than the ordinary sins and short-comings of the ordinary respectable and religious man. What, then, shall we say? Who will waver between these two men? Who can for a moment hesitate to rank the Pharisee higher than the publican? And yet it is our Lord's judgment—it is God's own verdict—that this man, this publican, this sullied, sin-stained, but withal penitent man, went down to his home justified rather than the highly respectable, highly respected, highly religious Pharisee. The answer is this—to know God is the beginning and the end of all wisdom; to know God is to think truly, is to act truly, is to live truly. Now, the Pharisee did not know God; he was altogether at fault in his ideas of God; he was on the wrong line, and however far he might go on that line he would be no nearer to God. On the other hand, the publican had taken the right direction; he might be still very far from a thorough knowledge of

God; but his ideas of God, however imperfect, were right as far as they went. Let us look into this matter a little more closely.

There are two ways of regarding God. We may look upon Him as a taskmaster, or we may look upon Him as a righteous Father. The first way is hopelessly, irretrievably wrong; the second way alone will lead us to Him. We may look upon Him as a taskmaster. What then? He sets before us a definite piece of work to do. If we do it, well and good; we escape blame; we get our pay. It is give and take; certain things are to be done, and certain other things are to be left undone. There the matter ends. This is what is meant by justification by works. It is a mere question of bargaining. We treat with God as a workman would treat with an employer of labour; we look upon Him as one of ourselves, a little more powerful, a little more exacting, a little more stern, but still as one of ourselves—a man, magnified indeed, but a man still, with whom we can stipulate and bargain and haggle about the amount of work to be done. That is the error, the fatal error, of the man in the parable who hid his one talent in the earth. " I feared thee, because thou art an austere man "—not, " I loved thee," not "I reverenced thee," not "I worshipped thee," but "I feared thee." It was apprehension, it was dread—nothing else; no affectionate yearning, no childlike outpouring of the heart, no seeking after the Father's embrace. "Thou art an austere man"—a hard man; yes, a taskmaster, and a rigorous taskmaster, too. "Lo, there thou hast that is thine"—not a little more, nor a little less—"thou hast that is thine." "Nay, everything is Mine. Heaven and earth are Mine; infinite righteousness and infinite truth, and infinite purity and infinite love, are Mine. Thou canst never give Me that is Mine." And so it is with the Pharisee in our parable, though the type of character is somewhat different. Fasting is enjoined, therefore he fasts; tithes are commanded, therefore he pays tithes. Not a moment is deducted from the fasting, not a penny is withheld from the tithes. He will be all safe; he does his work and he claims his pay. Of those boundless reaches of mercy, of truth, of love, which lie beyond all definite precepts, all specific duties, he thinks nothing and he knows nothing; of the infinity of God, he is wholly ignorant; of God's absolute righteousness, of God's limitless goodness, he has not a thought;

therefore he is satisfied; therefore he despises others. If he had any, even the faintest, conception of these, he could not be so complacent, he could not compare himself advantageously with others. To him who sees this infinity of God boasting is altogether excluded; he is fain to call himself an unprofitable servant. Ah, yes! it all springs from that one original root of falsehood, that perverse, fatal idea of the relations of man to God—so much pay for so much work—haggling between employer and employed—conflict, in an exaggerated form, between capital and labour once more.

But the true way to regard God is to look upon Him as a righteous Father, to see His righteousness first, and then to see His fatherly love. To see His righteousness, the awe, the beauty, the majesty, the holiness, the glory of His righteousness! Have we caught only a faint, transient glimpse of it? What then? What becomes of our righteousness, our merit, our self-satisfaction, our self-complacency? What miserable, besmirched, filthy tatters do the very best of them seem if only for a moment the skirts of His glistening raiment have crossed the field of our vision, the glory of Him who is clothed in righteousness. Do we thank God, can we thank God now, that we are not as bad as other men are? Nay, thank Him for His opportunity, thank Him for His mercy, thank Him for His forbearing patience, but thank Him not where thanksgiving is a mere cloak of self-complacency. No; you cannot compare yourself with another now; you see only your own sin, you can measure only your own unworthiness now, or, rather, it appears far beyond measuring to you. Your righteousness and this man's unrighteousness, your good and this man's evil—what difference is there between them in the presence of God's infinite holiness, that great leveller of all human gradations?

> "For merit lives from man to man,
> And not, O God, from man to Thee!"

Ah, yes, Lord! I can see two things, and two only: Thy righteousness, my sinfulness, these and nothing else.

But we must look not only to God's righteousness: we must look to His fatherly goodness also. We have beheld the heinousness of our sin in the mirror of His holiness; we must now behold the grace of our forgiveness in the light of His love,

His fatherly love. And have we not full and perfect assurance that His love will never fail us? What else is the meaning of His great, His inestimable gift to man of His only-begotten Son, to take His flesh upon Him and to die for us? By the infinity of His gift He would show us that His love is infinite also—nothing less; and we do Him a wrong, a cruel wrong, if we approach Him as a taskmaster, as a tyrant, as "a hard and austere man;" we blaspheme His fatherly goodness. Have we sinned, and shall we go to Him as to a taskmaster? What consolation, what forgiveness, what hope of either here? Nay, rather we will seek Him as the prodigal son sought Him; we will go to Him as to a father; we will address Him as a Father; we will betake ourselves to Him with a child's penitent heart, with a child's trusting soul, with a child's yearning embrace, and He will have compassion on us, will hasten to meet us, though we may be yet a great way off, and we shall be locked once more in His everlasting arms.

Do you think, can you think, that the sense of His infinite love will make you reckless, will make you indolent, will make you presuming? Did love, true love, truly felt, ever have this effect? Nay, just in proportion as you appropriate it, as you realise it, it will quicken, it will stimulate, it will purify, it will inspire you; it will transform your whole being into its own perfections from glory to glory. God's love is the beacon star in the sky, arresting, attracting, guiding, luring us forward on the heavenly path; the love of Christ—not our love for Him, but His love for us—the love of Christ, constrains us, binds us hand and foot, and drags us onward with the cords of a man. The publican did see this, at least in part. He saw God's righteousness in all its tremendous majesty, and he abased himself before it; he saw God's fatherly love only dimly as yet, but yearned for it. Therefore, though he was yet a great way off, God ran to meet him; and so, notwithstanding his sin, he went down from the temple that day "justified rather than the other."

One more thought is suggested by the parable. Prayer is the test of character. So it was with this Pharisee and this publican; so it must ever be, from the nature of the case. Prayer is the confronting of self with God; prayer is the communing with God; prayer is the laying bare of the soul before God. Thus prayer proves the realities of a man's being. As a man prays, so he is. He who has learned to pray aright has learned to live aright. The first and the last lesson of our lives, the first and the last desire of our hearts, the first and the last petition on our lips must be with us, as it was with the disciples of old, " Lord, teach us to pray"; and to the old question the old answer will be vouchsafed now, as then, "Our Father, which art in heaven." "Our Father." The sense of God's Fatherhood, as manifested in Christ, flooding our hearts, and dominating our lives—this is the beginning and the end of all theology; there is nothing before and nothing after this. Therefore, holy Father, we beseech Thee for Thy dear Son's sake, teach us all, this night and ever, to pray; teach us to know Thee, the only true God, and Jesus Christ, whom Thou hast sent; teach us so to pray that we may be found among the company of those faithful people who worship not a god of their own making, not a taskmaster, not a tyrant, not "a hard and austere man," but worship Thee, 'worship the Father in spirit and in truth."

OUR CITIZENSHIP.*

"Our conversation is in heaven."—PHIL. iii. 20.

A BETTER translation is "Our citizenship is in heaven."

We are all proud of our country. We delight to think of ourselves as belonging to a land on which whoever sets his foot is free. We reflect with satisfaction that we are citizens of a great empire on which the sun never sets. We feel that we have derived a very real advantage from our position; the glory of our past history is somehow reflected upon us. We think with pride of how freedom has "broadened slowly down, from precedent to precedent." We cherish the recollection too, of the most glorious scenes in our history, as if, somehow, they were part and parcel of ourselves. We feel as of one family, with its long roll of illustrious statesmen, generals, men of science, — our Shakespeare, Bacon, Newton, Wellington, Nelson, Hampden, Pitt, Canning,—

* Preached at Manchester Cathedral, at annual meeting of Additional Curates Society, on Tuesday, November 1st, 1887.

that these are our fellow-citizens. Their renown is our renown. It is a great thing to extend our range of view beyond ourselves, beyond our own households, our parish, and our own neighbourhood, and yet to feel that there is a bond of union still; that we are members of a great family, citizens of a great kingdom, unique in her great world-empire. The inspiration of this thought, which the recent Jubilee celebration has emphasised, makes us higher, nobler, larger than ourselves. It drives out all the pettiness of character and all the narrowness of view. True patriotism is a very noble and ennobling sentiment. To be ready to do and to suffer, if need be to die, for our country, what broad elevation of soul is there not in a temper like this?

St. Paul felt all this. He was proud of the city, of the nation to which he belonged. He was proud of the city in which he first saw the light. We cannot mistake his tones here. "I am a citizen of no mean city." This Tarsus, in which he was born, stood second to none as a seat of learning in his time. He was proud, also, of his nationality. Here, again, we cannot mistake the feeling which underlies his language. "Of the stock of Israel, of the tribe of Benjamin." "Are they Hebrew? So am I. Are they the seed of Abraham? So am I." He, too, was the son of the patriarchs; he, too, was the heir of the promises; he, too, had his portion among the twelve tribes that served God day and night. Was he not descended from the one favoured tribe which had given its first king to Israel, which had remained faithful to the house of David when all the others revolted; which ever marched in the van of the Lord's host when the armies went out to battle? "After thee O Benjamin!" No taint of foreign admixture had sullied the purity of his blood. He was "an Hebrew of the Hebrews." No concession to foreign excitements, and no relaxation of national rites, had ever compromised his position. He was a Pharisee of the Pharisees. Of all these things he might well be prouder than the proudest. Albeit he paused and kept down all his pride; he counted all as loss for the excellency of the knowledge of Christ Jesus his Lord. And lastly, he was proud of his position as a member of that great empire which stretched out her hand into every clime, and carried her citizens into all quarters of the globe. Here again his language tells its own tale. "They have beaten us openly, uncondemned, being Romans, . . . and now do they thrust us out privily." " Is it lawful for you to scourge a man that is a Roman, and uncondemned ? "

Yes; it was a magnificent privilege this, that a man, whosoever he might be, could claim the immunity, the protection, the deference which was everywhere accorded to a citizen of Rome ; to feel that he was a solitary, homeless wanderer, and had nevertheless at his back all the power, and all the prestige, and all the majesty of the mightiest empire that the world had ever seen. But however natural, and in some sense justifiable, may be this pride in ourselves, or in St. Paul, we are reminded by the text that he and we alike are citizens of a far larger, wider, more magnificent, more powerful, more enduring empire. For which we have every reason to feel, not indeed pride, not self-satisfaction, not vainglory, but perpetual thanksgiving, and benediction to the Author and Giver of all good things. Our citizenship is in heaven.

"Our citizenship." In the familiar version the word is rendered "conversation," *i.e.*, " walk of life." But it means very much more than this ; it points us out as members of a commonwealth, citizens of a polity, subjects of a kingdom, in

Our Citizenship. 161

which we have special interests, special responsibilities and functions. So, again, the Apostle tells the Ephesians, now converted from heathenism to the knowledge of Christ—"Ye are no more strangers and foreigners, but fellow-citizens with the saints."

"Fellow-citizens with the saints." You and they, bound together as members of one great nationality, with common duties, common sympathies, common aims, citizens of a kingdom of which the noblest and most powerful earthly empires are only faint types and shadows, a kingdom which shall never end. Yes!

> "Two worlds are ours, 'tis only sin
> Forbids us to descry
> The mystic heaven, and earth within,
> Plain as the sea and sky."

And so we need to strive this day to pierce through the veil, that so we may realise this our heavenly citizenship.

On this festival of All Saints, before all other days in the year, we are invited to enter into the Holy City, to dwell on the glories of the unseen world, to commune with the beatified servants of God of all ages and all countries, and to gather inspiration and truth and refreshment for our daily tasks in life ; to pierce through the veil, the dark impenetrable mist which shrouds the unseen world. Yet ever and again this veil is lifted for a moment, ever and again we are made to feel, by some startling occurrence, how narrow is the screen which separates the seen from the unseen, the material from the spiritual, the world of time from the world of eternity. Ever and again the stern monitor death rises up an unbidden guest, an unwelcome spectre in the midst of our worldliness and self-complacency, scaring us with the suddenness of the apparition. Mystery of mysteries, when valuable lives are suddenly cleft asunder, while so much that is worthless, and worse, is spared. Mystery quite insoluble if this were all, if the region beyond the grave were a mere vacuum ; if men were dust and nothing more ; if there were no immortality, no heaven, nothing to live for, nothing to work for, nothing to die for. Warnings these, solemn and thrilling, if only we have ears to hear, that this life is not our true life, that here we are strangers and pilgrims, that heaven is our only abiding house, that we are fellow-citizens of the saints.

"Fellow-citizens of the saints." Think for a moment how much is implied in this. What a vast assemblage, what a glorious companionship is that in which you and I, with our frailties, our shortcomings, our self-seeking, our worldliness, our distrust, our faithlessness, are fain boldly to claim a place! All those glorious spirits, venerable patriarchs, righteous kings, rapt seers, glorious psalmists, who lived and wrought and suffered in the ancient days in the hope of a better promise; men "who through faith subdued kingdoms, wrought righteousness, . . . of whom the world was not worthy;" all those apostles and teachers who, kindling their torches at the sacred fire, the glory of the Eternal Son Himself, carried the light of the gospel into all lands, giving up everything for Christ, offering to lose their lives, that by losing them they might find them. All these martyrs and doctors of later ages who handed down the sacred treasure through successive generations, amidst the fire of persecution and the confusion of barbarism and the darkness of idolatry, rejoicing to be devoured by hungry lions and to die at the stake. Polycarp, calm and brave as his flesh quivered in the flame; Chrysostom, with his flowery eloquence; Augustine, with his piercing insight and force,—these share, too, in this glorious company whose names live in history. And others, true saints of God, though they appear not in the calendar of any Church; men and women from the rigour of whose lives succeeding generations have their inspiration and strength; all whose holiness and purity, whose courage and self-sacrifice, whose gentleness and meekness, whose loving charity have been a never-failing fountain of refreshment to the weary pilgrim in the thirsty wilderness of the world. And others, too, there are whose memories shall perish not, though they have left no name in history, but whose brows, nevertheless, God Himself will crown with a halo of everlasting glory. Poor, despised, unknown artisans and peasants, weak women and feeble children, martyrs in the martyrdom of daily life, saints in the saintliness of homely duty, throngs innumerable of every nation and kindred and people and tongue, clothed with white robes and palms in their hands, standing before the Throne of God, and serving Him day and night in His temple.

And others again there are, unknown to the world, but well known to you and to me, saints of our home, of our school, of our college, of our workshop, of our office. Voices which were silent years ago mingle in our ears still, the hands crumbling in the dust have left a pressure that is still felt, the eyes long since glazed in death ever now and again are bright for us. The mother at whose knees we lisped our infant prayer, the child whose innocent prattle soothed our cares and sweetened our lives, the husband or wife who was part of our existence, the friend "more than my brothers are to me," whose nobleness and purity, whose unselfishness was the good genius and the pole star of our lives. These all are there, with these we hold communion, with these we walk and talk once more to-day as of old. This is the citizenship of which the text speaks, of which the day reminds us, more glorious beyond comparison than any earthly society which eye hath seen or of which ear hath heard. For these manifold and great gifts of which the season reminds I beseech you this afternoon give a worthy thankoffering. No, that cannot be, that is impossible, but if not worthy, at all events large and liberal.

And what fitter object can I set before you than the support of a society whose sole aim is the enrolment of citizens into the kingdom of God, the enlargement of the communion of saints? The jubilee year of our sovereign's reign is the jubilee year of this society. It was only in the process of formation when our Queen ascended the throne; one of her earliest acts was to give her name as its patron. It was a right queenly act, for of all the blessings for which during the half-century the nation has poured forth its thanksgiving at the Jubilee festival, surely none has been greater or more enduring than those which have been conferred through the instrumentality of this society.

For what was the state of things at the beginning of this period? Enormous arrears of spiritual work to be overtaken; everywhere great masses of people in our large centres absolutely beyond the reach of Church ministration; the population about to increase "by leaps and bounds." During these fifty years the society has made not less than 21,000 grants to poor parishes here and there, the amounts being on an average about £50. It has paid out in this way more than £1,000,000. And this sum has been met by £1,000,000 from contributions coming in from elsewhere; so that through its beneficent agency not less than £2,000,000 have been contributed for the increase of clerical ministration in the poor and populous districts of the land.

But these £2,000,000 are far from being an adequate standard of its beneficent effects. The planting down of an efficient clergyman in a poor district means the revival of Church work there; means, frequently, the erection of a church and schools; means the creation of a new parochial machinery. And thus the work of this Society is borne through in a thousand various ways which it is impossible to reckon up or to tabulate.

But you will ask, What is it doing at the present moment? If its operations have been thus effected in the past, does it still maintain its efficiency? I am glad to be able to give this question an answer which none can gainsay. It never was doing a greater work, nor as great a work, as at this very time. It gives grants to more than 850 curates; these grants amount to more than £56,000 per annum, and this sum is met by about the same amount from other sources. Thus more than £100,000 a year is expended directly through its instrumentality to the ministerial staff of the Church. But it is not only the extent of its operations which constitutes its claim on the support of all loyal churches. The principle also of this administration demands their allegiance. I do not desire to say one word of disparagement about other societies which are constituted on a broader or a narrower base. All are welcome; all are doing good service. There is work enough and to spare for all. But this association appeals to loyal English churchmen by the very fact that its foundation principle is neither wider nor narrower than the Church it represents. It imposes no tests which the Church does not impose; it requires no assents which the Church does not require. Within its limits the individual opinions of the clergymen count for nothing; the needs of the parish are all in all. But if it has this paramount claim on all loyal churchmen, surely it appeals to none more strongly than to the churchmen of this great city. No diocese draws so large an amount from it as this of Manchester; I believe I am right in saying that no city receives more material aid from it; and remembering this I cannot think that you will lay yourselves open to the charge of spiritual ingratitude, of all ingratitude the worst. Let there, then, be a liberal response to the appeal this afternoon, liberal in the sense that every giver will feel his gift ; that it will cost him some real sacrifice.

At this season, when we are especially called to glorify God in His saints, you cannot afford to be niggardly. Such niggardliness drags you downward, and is never more out of place than when you are attempting to lift up your souls to dwell in the heavenly city where Christ sits enthroned at the right hand of God. Ever, indeed, you need to be reminded of your heavenly citizenship amidst the cares and turmoil of life. It is with you as with the law-giver of old when he descended from the mount. The radiance will vanish from your countenance only too soon as you mingle with the busy crowd below. And you too, like Moses, will need to reappear ever and again at the mountain of God, that, standing face to face with the Eternal Presence, you may gather once more in your city the rays of the invisible glory.

AMBITION.

"I can do all things through Christ that strengtheneth me" [Πάντα ἰσχύω ἐν τῷ ἐνδυναμοῦντί με, "I have strength for all things in Him that empowereth, enableth me"].—PHIL. iv. 13.

AMBITION, the love of power, the thirst after influence—its use and its abuse, its true and its false aims—this is no unfit subject for consideration from a University pulpit.

Ambition in some form or other is an innate craving of man. All men desire power, they cannot help desiring it. The desire is as natural to them as the desire of health. Power and influence occupy the same place socially that strength and vigour of limb do physically. Other desires, though veiled under various disguises, resolve themselves ultimately into a love of power. Knowledge is power. The cultivated intellect has a command of the resources of the universe. The selfish exaggeration of this feeling is a testimony to the underlying fact. The self-satisfied soul congratulates herself that she is

> "Lord over nature, Lord of the visible earth,
> Lord of the senses five."

She communes with herself—

> "All these are mine,
> And let the world have peace or wars
> 'Tis one to me."

Again, money is power. A man desires wealth, not for the sake of the stamped metal or the printed paper in themselves. These represent to him a command of resources. The miser, indeed, by base indulgence forgets the end in the means. In his own domain he resembles the spurious mathematician to whom the letters and symbols are all in all, who sees in them so many counters and nothing more, who is blinded to the eternal relations of space and number which they represent. But traced back to its origin, the miser's love of money is a love of power.

Ambition, emulation, rivalry plays a highly important part in the education of the world. We cannot shut our eyes to its splendid achievements. In politics, in social life, in mechanical inventions, in literature and art, its stimulus has produced invaluable results. If ambition has been the last infirmity, it has also been the initial inspiration of many a noble mind. If by ambition angels fell, by ambition men have risen. It has heightened their ideal and drawn them upwards from lower to higher. If it is chargeable with the worst evils which have devastated mankind, it must be credited also with the most splendid advances in human progress and civilization.

Ambition has its proper home in a University. Ambition is the life of this place. What would Cambridge be without its honourable emulations, its generous rivalries? Body and mind alike feel the stimulus of its presence. Remove this stimulus, and the immediate consequence will be torpor and degeneration and decay. The athletic ambitions and the scholastic ambitions of the place, each in their own province, are indispensable to its health and vigour.

To one who, revisiting the scenes amidst which the best years of his life were spent, asks himself what topic may be fitly handled in this pulpit, the subject of ambition will naturally suggest itself. The University has lived through a period of exceptional restlessness and change during the last three decades—change far more considerable than during the preceding three centuries. Yet the spirit and life of the place are unchanging. It is the ceaseless orderly march of a mighty army moving forward. Cross it where you will along the line, the gesture, the tread, the uniform, is the same; the faces only are different. It is the broad, silent, ever-flowing river, changeless, yet always changing. Wave succeeds wave; you gaze on it at intervals; not one drop of water remains the same; and yet the river is not another. The main currents of University life are the same now as thirty years ago. Its moral and social condition is mainly, we may say, the resultant of two divergent forces, its friendships and its emulations. It is the latter alone that I purpose considering this afternoon.

I speak to you, therefore, as to ambitious men. Those only are beyond hope who have no spirit of emulation, no craving after excellence—those only, in short, who are devoid of ambition. I invite you, therefore, to be ambitious. Only I ask you to purify your ambition, to consecrate it, to direct it through worthy channels and to worthy aims. I desire to show you the more excellent way.

If, indeed, ambition has achieved splendid results, it can only have done so by virtue of splendid qualities. It must contain in itself true and abiding elements, which we cannot afford to neglect. Thus it involves a love of approbation. This cannot be culpable in itself. As social beings, we have sympathies and affections which lie at the very roots of our nature ; and the desire of approval is inseparably intertwined with these. Who would blame the child for seeking to win its mother's good opinion ? But the principle cannot be limited to this one example. It is co-extensive with the whole range of our social relations. The end sought is commendable. Only it may be discredited and condemned by the means taken to attain it ; as, for instance, if we disguise our true sentiment, or withhold a just rebuke, or connive at wrongdoing, or sacrifice a noble purpose, for the sake of standing well with others. It is then, and then only, that the praise of men conflicts with the praise of God. Again, ambition implies a spirit of emulation. Neither is this wrong in itself. If it were, this University would stand condemned root and branch. Emulation is not envy ; emulation is not jealousy ; emulation does not seek to injure or rob another. An apostle avows it to be his aim to "provoke to emulation." This provocation—this stimulus of comparison and contrast —is an invaluable influence. We measure ourselves with others ; we see our defects mirrored in their excellences ; our ideal is heightened by the comparison. Thus there gathers and ferments in us a *discontent* with ourselves—not indeed, if we are wise, with our capacities, not with our opportunities, not with the inevitable environments of our position, but with the conduct of that personality which is free to discipline, to mould, to direct, to develop our endowments. This dissatisfaction with self is the mainspring of all high enterprise and all moral advancement.

But the chief element in ambition is the pursuit of power. The consciousness of power gives a satisfaction quite independently of the exercise of power. Whatever form the power may take—whether intellectual eminence, or social influence, or physical strength, it is a thing which man desires, which he cannot help desiring, in and for itself. It is a seed of God's own planting—a germ of splendid achievements, if rightly trained and cultivated. It is only culpable in its excesses and deviations. By our very constitution we feel a happiness in making the best of ourselves, as the phrase runs—in developing and improving our faculties, irrespective of any ulterior results. But a faculty improved is a power gained.

Brothers, I desire before all things to kindle in you a lofty ambition to-day. Therefore, I have striven to justify ambition to you as God's very precious gift. I wish—God helping me—to inspire you with that inward dissatisfaction, that discontent with self, that ceaseless, sleepless craving after higher things, which gives you no rest day or night, because it pursues an ever-receding goal. I would stimulate in you that high spirit of emulation which, fermenting and seething in your hearts, impels you to unknown enterprises. I ask you to pray for power, to pursue power, to grasp at power, with all the force and determination which you can command.

How can I do otherwise? Are not you the men, and is not this the season, for the handling of such a topic?

Are not you the men? Who among you has not felt, at one time or another, the spark of a divine fire kindling within you? Who has not yearned with an intense, if momentary, yearning to do something worthy, to be something worthy? Youth is the hey-day of hope, of enthusiasm, of lofty aspiration. You have felt that there was within you a latent power, a heaven-born capacity, which ought to work miracles, if it were not clogged by self-indulgence, or cowed by timidity, or choked by sloth and indulgence.

Are not you the men? As I have said to such

audiences before, so I say to you now. You do not know, you cannot know, with what reverence—a reverence approaching to awe—older men regard the glorious potentiality of youth, in all the freshness of its vigorous life, with all the promise of the coming years. Our habits are formed; our career is defined; our possibilities are limited. The wide sweep of moral victory, still open to you, is closed to us for ever. But what triumphs may you not achieve, if you are true to yourselves? What instruments may you not be in God's hands, if only you will yield yourselves to Him—not with a timid, passive, half-hearted acquiescence, but with the active concentration of all your powers of body and soul and spirit?

And again I ask, is not this the time? The first volume of your life's history is closed. A clean page lies open, and with what writing shall it be filled? This is the great crisis of your life. These earliest few weeks of your University career, with which perhaps you are trifling, which you are idling thoughtlessly away, are only too likely to determine for you what you shall be in time and in eternity. It is the great crisis, but it is also the signal opportunity. Thank God, this is so; for the two do not always coincide. As the great break in your lives, it is the great season for revision, for repentance, for amendment, for the strong resolve and the definite plan. The old base associations must be abandoned; the old loose habits must be cured; the old indolence shaken off; and the old sin cast out and trampled under foot. Never again will such a magnificent opportunity be given you of rectifying the past; for never again can you reckon on the leisure, the privacy, the aids and environments, needed by one who is taking stock of his moral and spiritual life.

Who would not shrink from the responsibility of addressing you at such a crisis? And yet I speak boldly to you. Do I not know that though the hand of the swordsman is feeble, yet the weapon itself is powerful—keener than any two-edged sword? Am I not assured that though the preacher's words may be feeble, faltering, desultory, without force and without point, yet God may barb the ill-fledged, ill-aimed shaft, and drive it home to the heart? It is possible that even now the live coal from the altar may be brought by the winged seraph's hand, and laid on the sinful lips. I have undertaken to glorify the power of God, and to hold it up to you as your truest goal. How can I hope for a hearing, if I begin by distrusting it where I myself am concerned?

It is here, then, that I bid you seek and find the true aim of your ambition—in realising, appropriating, absorbing into yourselves, identifying yourselves with this power of God. It alone is inexhaustible in its resources and infinite in its potency. There is no fear here lest the conqueror of a world should sigh and fret because nothing remains beyond to conquer. If the craving is infinite, the satisfaction is infinite also. Star beyond star, world beyond world, will start out into view as your vision grows clearer, spangling the moral heavens with their glows. Πάντα ἰσχύω, " I can do all things." Πάντα ὑμῶν, " All things are yours." Yes, but this promise of limitless strength has its condition attached—ἐν τῷ ἐνδυναμοῦντί με, " In Him that empowereth me;" yes, but this pledge of universal dominion is qualified by the sequel ὑμεῖς δὲ Χριστοῦ, " Ye are Christ's."

How can we better realise this power of God than by taking St. Paul's statement as our starting-point? The Cross of Christ is "the power of God." The Cross is the central revelation of

God. The Cross has not unfrequently been preached as a narrow technicality which shocks the conscience and freezes the heart. It thus becomes a mere forensic subtlety. But the Cross of Christ, taught in all its length and breadth and height and depth—the Cross of Christ taught as St. Paul taught it—the Cross of Christ, starting from the Incarnation on the one side, and leading up to the Resurrection and Ascension on the other, contains all the elements of moral regeneration and of spiritual life.

(1) It is first of all a lesson of *righteousness*. It is the great rebuke of sin, the great assurance of judgment, the great call to repentance. Think —no, you cannot think, it defies all thinking—yet strive to think, what is implied in the human birth, the human life, the human suffering, the human death of the Eternal Word. Ask yourselves what condescension, what sacrifice, what humiliation is involved in this. Summon to your aid all analogies of self-renunciation which history records or imagination suggests. They will all fail you. No reiteration of the finite can compass the infinite. You are lost in awe at the contemplation. And while your brain is reeling with the effort, try and imagine the awe, the majesty, the

glory of a righteousness which could only thus be vindicated. Then, after looking upward to God, look inward into your own heart, and see how heinous, how loathsome, how guilty your guilt must be, which has cost such a sacrifice as this. God's righteousness—your sin,—these are brought face to face in the Cross of Christ.

(2) But, secondly, while it is a denunciation of sin, it is likewise an assurance of pardon. If the infinity of the sacrifice has taught you the majesty of God's righteousness, it teaches you no less the glory of His mercy. What may you not look for, what may you not hope for from a Father who has vouchsafed to you this transcendent manifestation of His loving-kindness? "He that spared not His own Son . . . how shall He not with Him also freely give us all things?" Is any one here burdened with the consciousness of a shameful past? Does the memory of some ugly school-boy sin dog your path, haunting and paralysing you with its importunity? You feel sometimes as if your whole life were poisoned by that one cruel retrospect. Brother, be bold, and dare to look up. I would not have you think your sins one whit less heinous. But if God's righteousness is infinite, so also is His mercy. The

Cross is reared before your eyes in this moral wilderness, where you are dying, where all are dying around you. Dare to look up. The bite of the serpent's fang is healed; the venom coursing through your veins is quelled; and health returns to the poisoned soul. Yes, and by God's grace it may happen that through your very fall you will rise to a higher life; that the thanksgiving for the sin forgiven will consecrate you with fuller consecration; and that the acute moral agony through which you have passed will endow you with a more helpful, more sympathetic, more loving spirit, than if you had never fallen.

(3) But again, the Cross of Christ is not only a condemnation of sin, not only a pledge of forgiveness; it is likewise an obligation of self-sacrifice. "God forbid," says St. Paul, "that I should glory save in the cross of our Lord Jesus Christ." But what next? Not "whereby I am saved in spite of myself," not "whereby I am spared all personal exertion," but "whereby the world is crucified unto me, and I to the world." This conformity to Christ's death, this crucifixion of self with Christ, always forms part of the doctrine of the Cross in St. Paul's teaching. The dying with Christ, the being buried with Christ, is the

absolute accompaniment of the atoning death of Christ. We cannot be at one with Christ unless we conform to Christ. The work done for us necessitates the work done by us. The potentiality of our salvation—of yours and mine—wrought through the Cross of Christ can only then become an actuality, when Christ's death is thus appropriated, realised, translated into action by us—by you and by me. But it remains still the work of God's grace. Human merit is absolutely excluded still, as absolutely as by the baldest and most unqualified doctrine of substitution.

(4) Fourthly and lastly, the Cross of Christ is a lesson of the regenerate and sanctified life. Dying and living, burial and resurrection, these in the Christian vocabulary are correlative ideas. The Crucifixion implies the Resurrection and the Ascension. The raising up on the cross demands the raising up from the grave, the raising up into heaven. The lifting up of the brazen serpent in the wilderness is a symbol alike of the one and the other. And as with Christ, so also with those who are Christ's. " If we died with Christ, we shall also live with him." Those only can be made conformable to Christ's resurrection who

have been made conformable to His death. The power of His resurrection is the counterpart to the power of His cross.

Herein, then—in the Cross of Christ—resides this power of God which is offered to you as the true aim of your ambition, inexhaustible, omnipotent, infinite. Will you close with the offer? Then reverence yourselves; believe in yourselves; consecrate yourselves.

Reverence yourselves. Begin with reverencing this your body. Reverence it as God's handiwork fearfully and wonderfully made. Contemplate it; yes, contemplate it with awe, if only for its marvellously subtle mechanism. But reverence it still more as the consecrated temple of God's Spirit. Do not neglect it; do not misuse it; before all things do not defile and desecrate it. Young men, the problem of social purity is thrown down for your generation to solve. Will you accept this challenge? The conscience of England is awakening to the terrible curse. To redress the crying social wrong, to raise womanhood from degradation and shame, to hold up to reverence the idea of a pure, chivalrous, manly manhood,—this is the crusade in which you are invited to enlist. Will you, as consecrated soldiers of the Cross, claim your part in the glory of this campaign? If so, the work must begin now, must begin in yourselves. There can be no success against the foe where there is disaffection and mutiny in the citadel.

Believe in yourselves; yet, not in yourselves as yourselves. Believe not in your strength, but in your weakness. Believe in God who dwells in you. Give full rein to your ambition. Trust this power of God. It will not stunt or mar, will not crush, will not annihilate your natural gifts—your social endowments, your political instincts, your intellectual capacities. It will only elevate, harmonize, inspire, purify them. Trust this power. There is nothing, absolutely nothing, which you may not do, if you will only trust it. Πάντα ἰσχύω, "I have strength for everything," everything in heaven and earth. You have youth, health, vigour, enthusiasm, hopefulness, everything on your side now. Seize the great opportunity which can never return.

Consecrate yourselves. Empty yourselves of yourselves, that you may be filled with God. Yield yourselves to Him, not with a passive acquiescence, a sentimental quietism, but with the earnest, energetic direction of all your faculties to this one end. A period must still intervene for most of you before the active independent work of life begins,—a period of discipline and waiting. Only by patience will you win your souls. But the self-dedication must be made at once, and it must be complete. Half-heartedness spoils the sacrifice. Postponement is perilous. The opportunity despised turns its back on you for ever. Consecrate, consecrate yourselves, body and soul and spirit, to God now, this night.

www.ingramcontent.com/pod-product-compliance
Lightning Source LLC
Chambersburg PA
CBHW031438160426
43195CB00010BB/780